Here lies the body of Michael O'Day
Who died maintaining his Right of Way.
He was right, dead right, as he sailed along,
But he's just as dead as if he'd been wrong.

CONTENTS

Introduction 9

How to Use this Book 10

Part One *What Every Boater Needs to Know*

Important Definitions 12
Do the Rules Apply to Me? 13
How Am I Responsible? 14
Does My Boat Need a Lookout? 15
What Is a Safe Speed? 15
Determining Risk of Collision 16
Action to Avoid Collision 18
In a Narrow Channel or Fairway 20
Traffic Separation Schemes 21
Overtaking 24
Power-Driven Vessels Meeting Head-On 26
Power-Driven Vessels Crossing 27
Two Sailboats Meeting 28
Mixed Vessel Types—The Pecking Order 28
Fog Situation 29
Sounds—Blow Your Own Horn 31
Lights—What Can They Tell You? 32
VHF Radio 42

Part Two *International and Inland Rules*

General 43
Rule 1 Application 43
Rule 2 Responsibility 45
Rule 3 General Definitions 46

SECOND EDITION

THE
One-Minute Guide
to the Nautical Rules of the Road

THE
One-Minute Guide
to the Nautical Rules of the Road

Charlie Wing

International Marine/
McGraw-Hill

Camden, Maine • New York •
Chicago • San Francisco •
Lisbon • London • Madrid •
Mexico City • Milan • New Delhi
• San Juan • Seoul • Singapore
• Sydney • Toronto

A United States Power Squadrons® Guide

The **McGraw·Hill** Companies

Copyright © 2006 International Marine

9 10 11 12 13 DOC/DOC 1 9 8 7 6 5 4 3 2

Library of Congress Cataloging-in-Publication Data
Wing, Charles, 1939

Library of Congress Cataloging-in-Publication Data

Wing, Charles, 1939–
        One minute guide to the nautical rules of the road / Charles Wing.
            p. cm.
        Rev. ed. of: Boating magazine's one minute guide to the nautical rules of the road. c1998.
        Includes index.
        ISBN 0-07-147923-6 (alk. paper)
        1. Inland navigation—Law and legislation—United States—Popular works.
        2. Rules of the road at sea—Popular works. I. Title.
        KF2566.Z9W53 2006
        343.7309'66—dc22   2006045746

Questions regarding the content of this book should be addressed to:
International Marine
P.O. Box 220
Camden, ME 04843

Questions regarding the ordering of this book should be addressed to:
The McGraw-Hill Companies
Customer Service Department
P.O. Box 547
Blacklick, OH 43004
Retail customers: 1-800-262-4729
Bookstores: 1-800-233-4726

Visit us on the World Wide Web at www.internationalmarine.com

Printed by R. R. Donnelley,
    Crawfordsville, IN
Design and page layout by
    Chilton Creative
Illustrations by Charlie Wing
Photo on title page courtesy Corbus.

Steering and Sailing Rules

Section 1 Conduct of Vessels in Any Condition of Visibility

Rule 4	Application	49
Rule 5	Lookout	49
Rule 6	Safe Speed	51
Rule 7	Risk of Collision	53
Rule 8	Action to Avoid Collision	55
Rule 9	Narrow Channels	57
Rule 10	Traffic Separation Schemes	60

Section 2 Conduct of Vessels in Sight of One Another

Rule 11	Application	62
Rule 12	Sailing Vessels	63
Rule 13	Overtaking	65
Rule 14	Head-on Situation	67
Rule 15	Crossing Situation	69
Rule 16	Action by Give-Way Vessel	71
Rule 17	Action by Stand-On Vessel	71
Rule 18	Responsibilities Between Vessels	73

Section 3 Conduct of Vessels in Restricted Visibility

Rule 19	Conduct of Vessels in Restricted Visibility	75

Lights and Shapes

Rule 20	Application	78
Rule 21	Definitions	79
Rule 22	Visibility of Lights	80
Rule 23	Power-Driven Vessels Underway	82
Rule 24	Towing and Pushing	83
Rule 25	Sailing Vessels Underway and Vessels Under Oars	85

Lights and Shapes *(continued)*

Rule 26	Fishing Vessels	*86*
Rule 27	Vessels Not Under Command or Restricted in Their Ability to Maneuver	*87*
Rule 28	Vessels Constrained by Their Draft	*88*
Rule 29	Pilot Vessels	*89*
Rule 30	Anchored Vessels and Vessels Aground	*89*
Rule 31	Seaplanes	*90*

Sound and Light Signals

Rule 32	Definitions	*90*
Rule 33	Equipment for Sound Signals	*91*
Rule 34	Maneuvering and Warning Signals	*92*
Rule 35	Sound Signals in Restricted Visibility	*95*
Rule 36	Signals to Attract Attention	*97*
Rule 37	Distress Signals	*97*
Rule 38	Exemptions	*98*

Annexes

Annex I: Positioning and Technical Details of Lights and Shapes	*100*
Annex II: Additional Signals for Fishing Vessels Fishing in Close Proximity	*107*
Annex III: Technical Details of Sound Signal Appliances	*108*
Annex IV: Distress Signals	*112*
Annex V: Pilot Rules (Inland Only)	*113*
Interpretive Rules	*116*
COLREGS Demarcation Lines	*117*
Penalty Provisions	*137*
Alternative Compliance	*141*
Waters Specified By the Secretary	*144*
Vessel Bridge-to-Bridge Radiotelephone Regulations	*145*
Legal Citations	*152*
Conversion Table	*153*

Index

Index	*154*

INTRODUCTION

The International Regulations for the Prevention of Collision at Sea (COLREGS) are the "Rules of the Road" on the water. These Rules, and the essentially identical United States Inland Rules, apply to all boats, regardless of type or size, on all seas and on most U.S. bays, inlets, rivers, and waterways connected to the sea.

In spite of the serious consequences of boating accidents, less than ten percent of boaters have an even rudimentary familiarity with the Rules. The International Maritime Organization estimates that over eighty percent of all boating accidents are due to human error and that most stem from the failure to comply with one or more provisions of the Rules.

The fact that most small boat operators lack a working knowledge of the Rules is understandable. Like most legal documents, the Rules appear to be quite complex. In translation, however, the Rules can be readily understood by anyone who knows port from starboard. We offer this little book as a painless introduction.

By law, all vessels of twelve meters or more in length that operate in U.S. Inland Waters are required to carry an up-to-date copy of the Rules. Courts have also ruled smaller boats negligent for not carrying them. This book, which includes all the annexes of the offical rules, satisfies that requirement.

The author, would like to thank numerous Coast Guard personnel for their input, Mr. Wesley Moore for his insightful review, and Jon Eaton for his patience.

HOW TO USE THIS BOOK

Inside the front cover you will find the One-Minute Guide, a "decision tree" indicating the action to be taken in any boating situation. Part One (pages 11–42) of the text presents the general principles of the Rules, and, beginning on page 19, follows the outline of the decision tree, helping you identify your situation. Throughout Part One, you will find marginal references to the appropriate Rule numbers. Part Two (pages 43–155) presents the full text of the Rules and offers further insight into their finer points.

The best way to learn the Rules is to begin following them. Read Part One thoroughly, then apply its principles to boating situations as they occur. You will soon find that the Rules make perfect (i.e., common) sense. Affix the One-Minute Guide Decision Tree to your cockpit as a ready reference, and you should never be confounded again.

Italicized text that appears in discussions of the Rules beginning on page 43 indicates where the Inland Rules differ substantially from International Rules (COLREGS).

Part One

What Every Boater Needs to Know

The purpose of the Rules is not, as is commonly thought, to grant one boat the right-of-way over another. The idea of a "right-of-way" fell out of favor as it became clear, through court cases, that avoiding a collision between two boats requires the participation of both parties. The purpose of the Rules is to present, in a situation where danger of collision between two boats exists, guidelines for the actions required of both. Under the Rules, one boat is designated the stand-on vessel; the other the give-way vessel (see page 12). These designations carry obligations for each vessel to act in a specified way to avoid collision.

It is important to note that the Rules never address situations involving more than two boats. Whenever the possibility of collision exists between more than two boats, common sense must be your principal guide.

Important Definitions

Vessel: anything that carries people or cargo on or in the water, including kayaks, personal watercraft, WIG craft and seaplanes, and super tankers.

Power-driven vessel: any vessel underway with an engine that does not fall into any of the other special categories defined below.

Sailing vessel: a sailboat underway with sails (not using an engine).

Vessel engaged in fishing: any boat fishing with equipment which limits its ability to maneuver (nets, trawls, etc.).

Vessel not under command: a vessel unable to maneuver as required by the Rules, due to mechanical breakdown or any other reason.

Vessel restricted in her ability to maneuver: a vessel that, due to the nature of her work, cannot maneuver easily. Examples include buoy tenders, dredges, dive boats, minesweepers, and tugs with difficult tows.

Vessel constrained by her draft: a vessel that may go aground if it deviates from its course. (Note that the Inland Rules do not contain this definition.)

Underway: not anchored, grounded, or otherwise attached to shore. A boat does not have to be moving either through the water or over the ground to be *underway*.

Restricted visibility: any condition that reduces visibility, including fog, heavy rain, snow, and smoke.

Give-way vessel: the vessel obligated to keep out of the way of the other.

Stand-on vessel: the vessel obligated to maintain its course and speed.

Wing-In-Ground (WIG) Craft: a multimodal craft which, in its main operational mode, flies in close proximity to the surface by utilizing surface-effect action.

Sailboat or Sailing Vessel?

When is a sailboat considered a "sailing vessel"? Cruising sailors often "motorsail"—that is, they run their engines to augment the wind. Rule 25(e) requires motorsailing sailboats (except those of less than twelve meters, under Inland Rules) to display a cone, apex down. Unfortunately, they rarely do so. You can usually tell that a boat is motorsailing by observing its exhaust.

Making the distinction between "sailing" and "motorsailing" is important because, under the Rules, running the engine turns a sailboat into a power-driven vessel. Be careful when crossing paths with a motorsailer, however. Many sailors think a sailboat is a "sailing vessel" as long as it has a mast and sails!

 ## Fishing Boat or Fishing Vessel?

When is a fishing boat not considered a "fishing vessel"? The Rules make it clear that when not engaged in the act of fishing, fishing boats have the same status as any power-driven vessel. But what about sport fishermen, lobstermen, and crabbers?

The distinction lies in the degree to which fishing gear hampers the maneuverability of a vessel. Trolling a light line does not hamper it; however, trawling or dragging a heavy net does. Although a lobsterman running to his next buoy is not hampered, when pulling up a string of traps with his hauler, he is effectively moored to the bottom.

Common courtesy dictates that you give these hardworking men and women a wide berth, so that they can concentrate on catching your dinner.

Do the Rules Apply to Me?

In a word—yes. The *International Regulations for the Prevention of Collision at Sea* (COLREGS) apply to all vessels, from kayaks to ocean-liners, on all of the oceans and bodies of water outside the magenta (red) Demarcation Line printed on charts. The United States Inland Rules apply on the Great Lakes, Western Rivers, waterways, and specific bays inside the Demarcation Line.

RULE
1

COLREGS or Racing Rules?

What happens when two sailboats collide while racing? A 1995 court case *(Juno SRL v. S/V Endeavor)* established that the International Yacht Racing Rules (IYRR), or whatever set of racing rules the sailboats are racing under, take precedence over the COLREGS during a race.

The two sailboats, *Charles Jourdan* and *Endeavor*, were racing in the Bay of St. Tropez. Approaching a mark, the *Jourdan* assumed it had the "right-of-way" under IYRR Rule 37.1, "a windward yacht shall keep clear of a leeward yacht." The *Endeavor* at first refused to keep clear. When she belatedly altered course to windward, her boom struck the *Jourdan*, causing $10,000 damage. The race committee, applying the IYRR rule, found the *Endeavor* at fault.

The *Jourdan* subsequently filed suit for damages in district court. The district court threw out the IYRR ruling, finding that the *Jourdan* had been an overtaking vessel under COLREGS Rule 13 and thus required to keep clear.

On appeal, however, the first circuit court overturned the district court's ruling, saying: "Nothing in their history, or in the public policy issues that led to their enactment, indicates that they (the COLREGS) were meant to regulate voluntary private sports activity in which the participants have waived their application and in which no interference with nonparticipating maritime traffic is implicated."

The case applies only to yachts participating in a race. It does not apply to other vessels in the vicinity that are not participating in the race. Thus, in a conflict between racing and nonracing boats, the COLREGS still rule.

How Am I Responsible?

Everyone having to do with the operation of your boat—its owner, master (person in charge underway), and crew—is responsible for obeying the Rules, as well as for using caution, good sense, and good seamanship. However, the Rules acknowledge that they cannot cover every conceivable situation. If absolutely necessary to avoid immediate danger, you are, in fact, required to break the Rules. In other words, use your head for the purpose intended, not as a hat rack.

Does My Boat Need a Lookout?

Absolutely! Your boat is required to maintain a lookout for the possibility of collision at all times and to use all available methods and equipment (eyes, ears, radio, and radar, if installed). Of course, if you are the only person on board, then you have to serve as master, crew, and lookout all at the same time. If there is more than one person aboard, however, the master should appoint a separate lookout.

RULE 5

 ## Do Single-Handed Sailors Have the Right to Zzzzz?

In a 1984 court case *(Granholm v. TFL Express)*, the court found a single-handed racer negligent for taking a thirty-minute nap.

The yacht, *Granholm*, was participating in a qualifying sail for a transatlantic race. With the boat on autopilot, and with all required navigation lights showing, the owner scanned the horizon for ships, set a thirty-minute timer, and went below for a nap. Meanwhile, the *TFL Express* was on autopilot, making eighteen knots; the mate was plotting her position, and the "lookout" was making tea. The *Express* came up from behind and ran the *Granholm* down.

The owner of the *Granholm* sued the *Express* for her failure to maintain a proper lookout (Rule 5), and for neglecting, as the overtaking vessel, her obligation to keep clear (Rule 13). The court agreed, but placed equal blame on the single-hander, saying, "The obligation to maintain a proper lookout falls upon great vessels and small alike."

In other words, if single-handed sailing prevents one from maintaining a "proper lookout," as defined by the Rules, then the very act is negligent. Single-handers beware.

What Is a Safe Speed?

You must never exceed a safe speed for the conditions. The Rules do not define "safe speed," but the courts have often interpreted it as the speed that would allow a boat to avoid collision. Factors you must consider include: visibility conditions, background lights, traffic intensity, maneuverability of your vessel, maneuverability of other vessels, wind and current, navigational hazards, depth of water, and the limitations of radar.

RULE 6

A Titanic Error in Judgment

Everyone knows the substance of the *Titanic* disaster, but do you know which single COL-REGS rule she broke?

Captain E. J. Smith, with over 2,000,000 miles under his keel, was given the honor of commanding the *Titanic* on her maiden voyage. Amidst great hoopla and newspaper stories citing the *Titanic* as proof of man's mastery over nature, she embarked from Southampton, England, on April 10, 1912, bound for New York. Her owners were anxious for her to show a good turn of speed on this, her very first outing. Captain Smith had another reason—this was to be his last trip before retiring.

There is little doubt that the pressure for a speedy Atlantic crossing clouded the judgment of the able Captain. On consecutive days, the *Titanic* ripped off 386 miles, 519 miles, then 546 miles. On the 14th, at 22½ knots, she was approaching her theoretical top speed of twenty-four knots.

Iceberg warnings began to come in from other vessels. At least eleven warnings were received, but iceberg warnings were common at this time of year. That Captain Smith received the warnings there is no doubt. Being a prudent mariner, he altered course slightly to the southwest.

At 11:40 P.M., the lookout in the crow's nest sounded the alarm, "Iceberg dead ahead!" The helm was put hard-a-starboard immediately. The *Titanic* responded—but not quickly enough. Less than forty seconds after the alarm, the iceberg struck the *Titanic* a glancing blow, punching a 300-foot series of holes beneath her waterline.

Have you guessed which COLREGS rule Captain Smith broke?

"Every vessel shall at all times proceed at a safe speed . . ." (Rule 6)

Determining Risk of Collision

RULE 7

Collision with another boat is possible when the compass bearing to it remains constant as your two boats converge. The rule specifically says that you must use all available means, including radar if you have it, to aid in this determination. Fortunately, for small boat operators without radar, a relative bearing sighted against a stanchion or other fixed part of your boat may substitute for a compass bearing, as long as you maintain constant course and speed. If there is any doubt at all, consider that collision is possible.

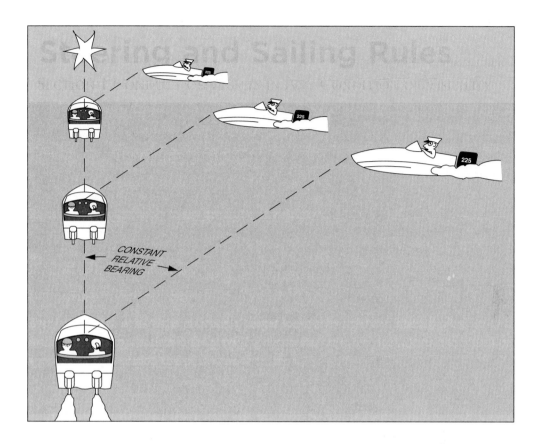

You Assumed What?

The collision of the *Stockholm* and the *Andrea Doria,* on the night of July 25, 1956, serves as a study in poor judgment. The Swedish-American *Stockholm* was on a course from New York City to the Nantucket Lightship, in conditions of good visibility. At the same time, the Italian *Andrea Doria,* operating in a dense fog, had passed the Lightship and was headed for New York. Captain Calamai of the *Andrea Doria* took his usual fog precautions: He positioned a lookout at the bow, closed all watertight hatches, and placed the engine room on alert. He reduced speed, but only from twenty-three to 21.8 knots, because he was running late and knew that any significant target would appear on his radar.

At 10:40 P.M., a target appeared. Captain Calamai, assuming the blip to be just a fishing boat, neglected to plot its course and speed, and further, ignored the time-honored custom of passing port-to-port. Had he known that the other vessel was coming nearly straight at him at nineteen knots, he probably would have taken early and substantial action by turning at least twenty degrees to starboard.

At 10:48 P.M., the third officer of the *Stockholm* saw on his radar a vessel (the *Andrea Doria*) twelve miles ahead. At ten miles, he plotted the twelve- and ten-mile relative positions and figured that the other vessel would pass one-half mile to one mile to his port. Since there was no fog where he was, he also assumed that he would soon see the other vessel's navigation lights. When, at four miles, there were still no lights, he assumed that either the other vessel's lights were broken, or that the vessel was a warship on maneuvers.

One minute later, the *Stockholm* entered the thick fog. Three minutes later, the *Stockholm*'s lookout sighted the *Andrea Doria*'s lights ahead to port, and the third officer turned his ship twenty degrees to starboard. At nearly the same instant, Captain Calamai spotted the *Stockholm*, and ordered the *Andrea Doria* to turn to port. The *Stockholm* struck the *Andrea Doria* on her starboard side, sending her to the bottom.

Captain Calamai's turn to port might be questioned, but the more important lesson to be learned from this accident is to never assume that you know what another vessel is doing.

Action to Avoid Collision

RULE 8

The give-way boat's action to avoid collision must be early and large enough to assure the stand-on boat that she is taking action. Given room to maneuver, changing course is better than changing speed because it is more immediately obvious to the other boat. A course change large enough to be obvious would present a different view of the give-way boat in daylight and different navigation lights at night. A large enough speed change would be throttling down to no-wake speed or even stopping.

The stand-on vessel is obligated to maintain course and speed. In a collision situation, the actions permitted or required of the stand-on vessel take place in four stages.

1. Before the risk of collision exists, either boat may maneuver as it pleases.
2. Once risk of collision exists, the stand-on boat must maintain its course and speed.
3. If it seems to the stand-on boat that the other boat is not going to keep out of the way, then she should sound the danger signal (five short blasts) and *may* take any action *except* a turn to port for a give-way boat on her port.
4. If the situation develops to the point where a collision can no longer be avoided by the action of the give-way boat alone, the stand-on boat is *required* to sound the danger signal and take the most effective action it can to avoid the collision.

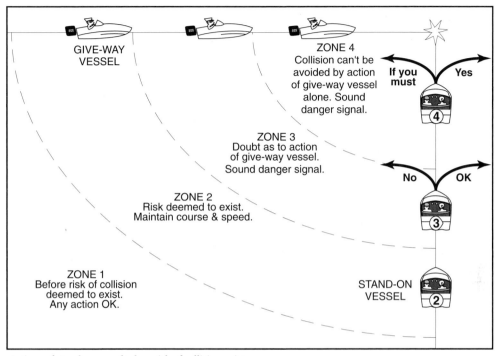

Actions of stand-on vessel when risk of collision exists

One-Minute Guide Decision Tree

The decision tree found on the inside front cover acts as a quick reference when approaching another vessel. If you can see the other boat, use the "In-Sight Situation" guidelines. Begin at the top and move down the left-hand column until you find the circumstance that pertains to you. If you are in an area of restricted visibility, use the bottom portion of the tree. The following information will help you identify your situation.

In a Narrow Channel or Fairway

RULE 9

A channel is a safe route between hazards, or a deeper route through shallow water. It is "narrow" when boats in it are severely limited in room to maneuver. A fairway is the thoroughfare between docks and piers in a harbor. In general, stay out of narrow channels and fairways that are trafficked heavily by large ships and tugs. When in a narrow channel or fairway, however:

+ Stay as close as possible to the starboard side.
+ Sailboats, fishing boats, and boats of less than twenty meters should stay clear of boats that are confined to the channel.
+ Do not cross the channel if it will interfere with a boat confined to the channel.
+ Do not anchor in the channel.
+ Sound a prolonged (four-to-six second) blast when approaching a bend or other obscured area. Boats approaching in the opposite direction should answer with the same signal.

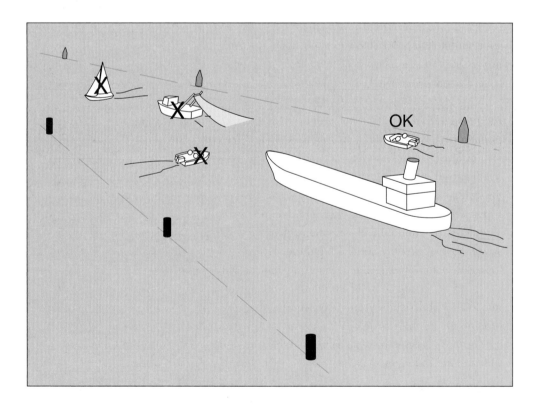

Traffic Separation Schemes

Traffic separation schemes (TSS) are inbound and outbound traffic lanes, divided by separation lines or zones, and printed in magenta on charts. Their purpose is to provide one-way lanes for large ships into and out of major ports. Between the traffic lanes and any adjacent land masses, you will usually find inshore traffic zones (labeled as such on your chart). Sailboats, fishing boats, and all boats under twenty meters (65'7") are free to use these inshore traffic zones, and in any case, are to stay clear of any ship using a traffic lane. If you must cross a traffic lane, do so quickly, far away from other vessels, and at a right angle to the flow of traffic.

Note that vessel traffic services, found only in the Inland Rules, are roughly equivalent to traffic separation schemes.

RULE 10

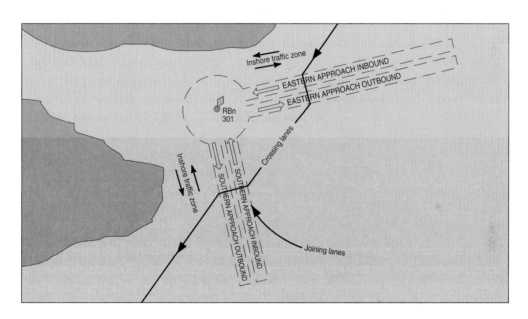

Kayaks and Other Speed Bumps

With the exception of the lighting requirements for Vessels Under Oars (Rule 25), there is no mention in either the COLREGS or the Inland Rules of rowboats, kayaks, canoes, or other human-powered vessels. The reason for this apparent oversight is that the Rules were developed for the purpose of preventing collision between ships on the high seas. It is only recently that one has seen kayaks on open waters. With the increasing appearance of what powerboaters are fond of calling "speed bumps," it is appropriate to consider how the Rules—or lack thereof—apply to these little craft.

First, which of the rules, if any, do apply to human-powered craft? Rules 1 through 11 and Rule 13 apply to all vessels, regardless of size or means of propulsion. Therefore, human-powered vessels must observe the general rules of responsibility, maintaining a lookout, not exceeding a safe speed, determining risk of collision, and taking proper action to avoid collision. Of particular importance, however, are Rules 9 and 10.

Rule 9 *Narrow Channels*

9 *(b)* "A vessel of less than twenty meters in length … shall not impede the passage of a vessel which can safely navigate only within a narrow channel or fairway."

Rule 10 *Traffic Separation Schemes*

10*(d)* "A vessel … of less than twenty meters in length … may use inshore traffic zones."
10*(j)* "A vessel of less than twenty meters in length … shall not impede the safe passage of a power-driven vessel following a traffic lane."

In other words, human-powered vessels should, whenever possible, stay out of channels used by large vessels.

Second, what about situations where the Rules are not specific? In discussions with U.S. Coast Guard personnel, two principles are repeatedly cited:

Maneuverability

Most of the Rules are based on the unstated principle of relative maneuverability; that is, the vessel having the greater ability to avoid collision under the circumstances is generally charged with keeping clear. Unfortunately, one cannot generalize and say that human-powered vessels are either more or less maneuverable than other craft. Kayaks and rowboats may be able to spin on a dime, but they are also slow. The relative maneuverabilities of a kayak and a larger vessel can thus depend on size, speed, wind, waves, current, depth of water, and navigation hazards, to name just a few.

Negligent Operation

The civil law concept of "negligent operation" can always be applied. Operating a vessel (or a motor vehicle, for that matter) without consideration for conditions, without reasonable precaution, and in violation of common sense, all constitute negligent operation.

When you combine these two principles, it is usually clear which of two vessels should stay clear in any given situation. A few examples should illustrate the point:

1. *High speed runabout on a collision course with a kayak.* Due to its much greater speed, the runabout could easily run down the kayak, regardless of evasive action by the kayak. The runabout should probably stay clear, as it must in an overtaking situation.

2. *Rowing dinghy crossing a harbor in a wind.* A rowing dinghy provides a common means of transportation between a moored or anchored vessel and shore. In a wind, progress can be slow enough that its operator cannot reasonably be expected to anticipate all of the vessel traffic he will meet on the way. Larger vessels should take this into account when applying the Rules. On the other hand, a freighter or tanker is large enough to be seen far in advance, in which case the dinghy operator should delay his crossing.

3. *Kayaker riding the bow wave of a larger vessel.* While great sport for the kayaker, it is also a distraction to the skipper of the larger vessel, who must consider the proximity of the kayak in maneuvering. Surfing another vessel's bow wave—at least in close proximity—is a clear case of negligent operation.

Look Out for Floating Objects

The following story illustrates the dangers of a small vessel sharing a narrow channel with larger vessels: On the evening of December 19, 1993, a pilot was lining up the bulk carrier *Sealnes* to pass under the Lions Gate Bridge on its way into Vancouver Harbor. At the same time, *Mr. Fission,* a thirty-foot dive tender, was headed out of the harbor. *Mr. Fission* was having engine trouble, so instead of crossing to the starboard side of the channel, as required, he decided to hug the port shore while he worked on his engine. The current in the channel was making 2.8 knots, but since it was running in a favorable direction, the captain decided not to anchor while the crew worked on the engine. Distracted by the engine repairs, the captain failed to notice that the strong current was drawing him out into the main channel.

The vessel traffic service (VTS) in Vancouver, which monitors and directs traffic in the controlled traffic lanes, advised the *Sealnes* of two radar targets in the channel ahead. The pilot assumed these to be the two tugs he expected to greet him. In fact, the tugs in question were so close to each other that they appeared on radar to be a single target; the second radar target was actually *Mr. Fission.*

The chief officer of the *Sealnes,* standing on deck, heard a noise over the starboard bow. When he looked, he saw *Mr. Fission,* upended, with her three crew in the water. The *Sealnes* had run down *Mr. Fission* without either vessel seeing the other.

What went wrong? The captain of *Mr. Fission* should have alerted the VTS and area traffic of his predicament, his location, and the fact that he was on the wrong side of the channel. He also should have maintained a proper lookout while repairing his engine. The pilot and crew of the *Sealnes* falsely assumed that the two targets reported by the VTS were the two tugs they were expecting. Rather than rely entirely on the VTS, they should have had their own lookout.

Overtaking

RULE
13

You are overtaking another boat when you approach it within the 135° arc of its sternlight. If there is any doubt as to whether you are overtaking, assume that you are.

When an overtaken boat must take action to be safely passed (as in a narrow channel), both boats must first reach agreement through sound signals (see page 31) or via VHF radio (Inland only). The burden is on the overtaking boat to steer clear until it is totally past and safely clear of the overtaken boat.

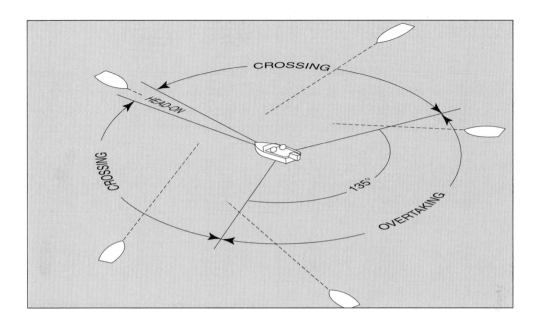

 ## Haste Makes Waste

A pleasure yacht and a large ferry were proceeding in the same direction down a narrow channel. To allow room for a third vessel, which was approaching from the opposite direction, the ferry passed the yacht close on the yacht's port side. The hydrodynamic effects caused by her large displacement and the suction of her propellers pulled the yacht into the side of the ferry, inflicting damage. Who was at fault?

- The ferry was an overtaking vessel and thus required to keep clear (Rule 13).
- The ferry should have reduced her speed in order to delay her passing (Rule 8).
- Since safe passage required action by the overtaken yacht, the ferry should have indicated her intention to pass and waited for the yacht to signal agreement (Rule 9).

"Is this not one of those cases of three or more vessels, and thus not subject to the Rules?" you might ask. Remember that when the Rules cannot be applied in a confusing situation involving more than two vessels you are to apply common sense. Here, common sense would dictate delaying the overtaking until the approaching vessel had safely passed, thus avoiding the three-vessel situation.

Power-Driven Vessels Meeting Head-On

RULE 14

Power-driven vessels meeting head-on should each alter course to starboard and pass port-to-port. Head-on is when you see: 1) in daylight, another boat headed nearly straight at you, or 2) at night, both sidelights or the masthead lights of the other nearly in line. If you have the slightest doubt whether the situation is head-on, assume that it is.

Exception: Power-driven vessels proceeding downbound on the Great Lakes and Western Rivers have the right-of-way over upbound boats and should propose the manner of passage via sound signals or VHF radio. Also, both upbound and downbound power-driven vessels have the right-of-way over all types of crossing vessels.

Who's on First?

On April 12, 1991, the 584-foot *Sersou* was downbound on the St. Lawrence River, moving at eight knots. At the same time, the 714-foot *Silver Isle* was upbound at 12.5 knots.

At 1803, the two vessels were about ⁹⁄₁₀ of a mile apart, and approaching a slight bend in the channel. Suddenly, the *Sersou* developed a swing to port. Whether the swing was due to helmsman error or to hydrodynamic effect is not known, but it was obvious enough to strike terror into the heart of the pilot of the *Silver Isle*, who had been expecting a normal port-to-port passing. The recorded conversation between the two French-speaking pilots reminds one of the Abbott and Costello "Who's on First?" routine:

(English Translation)

    1803:40 *(Sersou)* "Watch me closely, I'm hard-a-starboard."

    1803:53 *(Silver Isle)* "Are you OK to pass? Two whistles [under the Inland Rules, the signal for a starboard-to-starboard passing]."

    1803:59 *(Sersou)* "No, not two whistles, she's coming back."

    1804:03 *(Silver Isle)* "It's too late ... two whistles."

1804:07 *(Sersou)* "OK, two whistles"

1804:20 *(Sersou)* "Two whistles, eh?"

1804:21 *(Silver Isle)* "What did you say?"

1804:23 *(Sersou)* "What are you doing there, two whistles?"

1804:25 *(Silver Isle)* "Two whistles."

1804:28 *(Silver Isle)* "I'm going hard-a-port, hard-a-port."

1804:32 *(Sersou)* "I'm hard-a-port too."

[CRUNCH]

1804:54 *(Sersou)* "You told me ... you asked me to go to port."

What the recorded conversation doesn't show is that the *Silver Isle's* Officer of the Watch (OOW), not understanding French, became alarmed at the developing situation and ran to get the master. Since the OOW couldn't explain to the master what was happening, and, since the pilot was on the radio with the other pilot, the master unwittingly countered the pilot's instructions, ordering the *Silver Isle's* helm to starboard.

The lesson here is, clearly, the importance of communication in avoiding collision.

Power-Driven Vessels Crossing

A boat crossing your path from your starboard side should stand on (maintain course and speed), while a boat approaching you on your port side must give way. The give-way boat should not cross ahead of the stand-on boat. Remember, a stand-on boat on your starboard side sees your green "go" light, while a boat on your port side sees your red "stop" light. Conversely, you see the "go" light of a boat on your port, and the "stop" light of a vessel on your starboard. *Exception: On the Great Lakes and Western Rivers, any type of vessel crossing a river must keep out of the way of a power boat ascending or descending the river, regardless of port and starboard.*

RULE
15

Two Sailboats Meeting

RULE 12

First, a sailboat is a "sailing vessel" only when she is using her sails as her only source of propulsion. Next, the "tack" of a sailboat is the side opposite that on which the mainsail is carried (or, on a square-rigged vessel, the largest fore-and-aft sail). Given these definitions, the rule governing sailboats is simple:

+ When two sailboats are on different tacks, the boat on the port tack must keep clear.

+ When two sailboats are on the same tack, the boat to windward (upwind) must keep clear.

+ If a sailboat on a port tack is uncertain of the tack of an upwind sailboat, she must still keep clear.

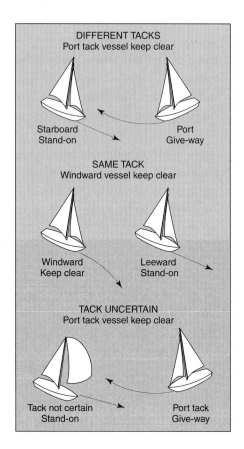

Mixed Vessel Types—The Pecking Order

RULE 18

Other than in a traffic separation scheme, a narrow channel, or an overtaking situation, you must observe a "pecking order." Find your boat in the illustration. You must stay clear of all vessel types above you; all vessel types below you must keep clear of you. Vessels not under command and vessels restricted in ability to maneuver share the top billing.

In order to claim privileged status, a vessel must display its appropriate shapes by day and lights by night. Failure to display such signals may get the privileged vessel in trouble; however, it will not let you off the hook if you tangle with them.

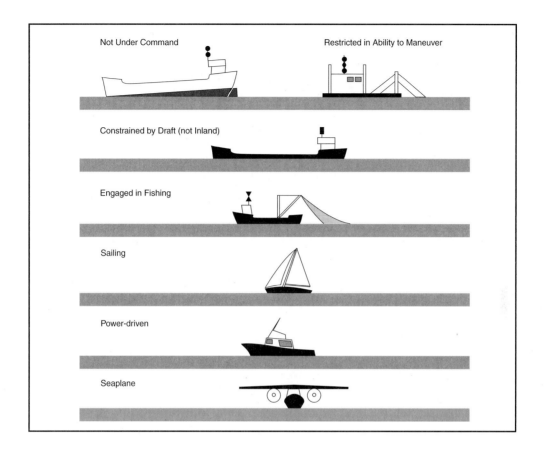

Fog Situation

All of the rules above assume that you see the other boat. In or near an area of restricted visibility, you must slow to a safe speed for the visibility, and sound fog signals. If you detect another boat by radar or by sound, you must evaluate the risk of collision. If risk does exist (decreasing range at constant bearing), you must take avoiding action, BUT DO NOT:

RULE
19

+ turn to port for a boat forward (unless you are overtaking it);
+ turn toward a boat abeam or aft your beam.

Unless you are absolutely certain that there is no risk of collision when you hear the fog signal of a boat forward, you must reduce your speed to bare steerageway or, if necessary, stop. Important: When (and if) your vessels become visible to each other, you both go back to the in-sight rules.

A Message from the Bridge

 Captain William Gribbin is a pilot for the harbor of Portland, Maine, one of the busiest oil ports on the U. S. East Coast. His job is to bring 800-foot tankers through the inner harbor to their berths. The message he sends to recreational boaters could come from the pilot or captain of any large vessel.

"I start popping Rolaids at Portland Head Light. That's when the acid really starts churning. Small boaters have no idea what it's like to maneuver an 800-foot tanker. They think, with all our power and radar and what not, that we have complete control—that we can turn to avoid them or even stop. Inside Portland Head Light, we are restricted to a speed of four knots. We have 12,000 horses, but at four knots, a loaded tanker takes a quarter of a mile and seven minutes to stop! Moreover, once we put the engines in reverse, we lose all steerage. To make an analogy, it's like pushing a thirty-foot Sea Ray with a one-horse trolling motor and steering with a shingle.

"We also have a blind zone up front. We can't see anything directly in front of us for about 600 feet. If a little guy disappears in front of us, I can only pop another Rolaid and pray that I won't see wreckage in our wake. Even if I could see that we were about to run him down, should I put the helm hard over and run the risk of dumping 100,000 barrels of crude oil into the environment? Sometimes, those are the only two choices I have.

"My favorite rule is the narrow channel rule, Rule 9. It says that sailboats, fishing boats, and boats of less than twenty meters shall not impede the passage of a vessel that can safely navigate only within a narrow channel. What does 'shall not impede' mean? To me it means:

+ Don't anchor in the channel.
+ Don't troll or drift in the channel.
+ Don't cross in front of me.
+ Don't pass between me and my tugs.
+ In fact, don't come within 250 feet of me!

"Now, about radar. Even on open waters, boaters should never assume that we see them. Sure, we have fancy radars—several, in fact. But you have to reflect the radar signal back in order for us to see you. Even with a good radar reflector, most small boats don't show up beyond a mile or two. Without a reflector, we're lucky to pick them up at a quarter mile. When waves kick up, we have to turn up the sea-clutter control to eliminate reflections from the nearest waves. We are essentially eliminating all reflections from close range. So much for kayakers! I have never seen a kayak on radar.

"I'm also amazed at how boaters use their radios. They have VHF, they have CB, they even have cell-phones. They call each other to see how the fishing is; they call to see if Joe remembered to bring the beer; but they never call us. All large vessels are required by the regulations to listen to VHF CH13 and CH16. If you want to tell us what you are doing or ask us what we are doing, please, please call us on CH13 or CH16!"

Sounds—Blow Your Own Horn

The Rules state that when a maneuvering action is required to avoid collision, the vessels involved must use sound signals to communicate their intentions. Since adoption of the Vessel Bridge-to-Bridge Radiotelephone Act, the more common practice under Inland Rules is to reach understanding on VHF radio CH13. The roots of the practice can still be heard, however, when captains propose passing on "one whistle" (port side–to–port side) or "two whistles" (starboard side–to–starboard side). The table below shows the sound signals required under both International and Inland Rules.

RULES 32–37

Vessels are also required to make sound signals when in or near areas of restricted visibility. These signals, identical for both International and Inland Rules, are shown below.

Maneuvering and Warning Signals in Sight
(• = one-second blast; — = four- to six-second blast)

INTERNATIONAL (action being taken)

MEETING OR CROSSING AND ACTION IS REQUIRED
(no answer required):

I am altering course to starboard	•
I am altering course to port	• •
I am operating astern propulsion	• • •

OVERTAKING IN A NARROW CHANNEL OR FAIRWAY AND ACTION IS REQUIRED
(agreement required before action):

I intend to overtake on your starboard	— — •
I intend to overtake on your port	— — • •
I agree to be overtaken	— • — •
Warning—I don't understand your intentions	• • • • •
Approaching a bend in a channel	—

INLAND (action proposed to be taken)

MEETING OR CROSSING WITHIN ½ MILE OF EACH OTHER AND ACTION IS REQUIRED
(agreement by same signal required):

I propose leaving you to port	•
I propose leaving you to starboard	• •
I am operating astern propulsion	• • •

OVERTAKING IN A NARROW CHANNEL OR FAIRWAY AND ACTION IS REQUIRED
(agreement by same signal required before action):

I propose overtaking on your starboard	•
I propose overtaking on your port	• •
I agree to be overtaken	• or • •
Warning—I don't understand your intentions	• • • • •
Approaching a bend in a channel or leaving berth or dock	—

Sound Signals in Restricted Visibility

(● = one-second blast; ▬ = four- to six-second blast. Repeat every two minutes, maximum.)

Power vessel making way	▬
Power vessel stopped	▬ ▬
Manned tow	▬ ● ● ●
Pilot vessel—optional	● ● ● ●
Not under command, restricted in ability to maneuver, constrained by draft, sailing, fishing, towing or pushing, fishing at anchor, restricted at anchcor	▬ ● ●

ANCHORED:

Less than 100 meters—ring bell rapidly for five seconds every minute

Greater than or equal to 100 meters—ring bell five seconds fore, then gong five seconds aft

Additional option	● ▬ ●

AGROUND:

Three distinct claps of bell + rapid five-second bell + three claps, all repeated at one minute

Vessel less than twelve meters option—any sound at two minutes

Lights—What Can They Tell You?

Definitions

The Rules specify the colors and arcs of visibility of navigation lights to be carried by each type of vessel, as described below:

Masthead light (also known as steaming light): white light on centerline showing forward from 22.5° abaft the beam on either side (225° arc).

Sidelights: green on starboard and red on port, each visible from dead ahead to 22.5° abaft the beam. On vessels less than twenty meters, the sidelights may be combined in one unit on the centerline.

Sternlight: white light at stern showing aft from 22.5° abaft the beam on either side (135° arc).

Towing light: the same as a sternlight, except for being yellow.

All-around light: a light of any color that shows 360° around.

Flashing light: a light flashing at a minimum of 120 times per minute.

Special flashing light (Inland): a yellow light flashing at fifty-seventy times per minute over an arc of 180–225°.

Range of Visibility

The Rules also specify minimum ranges of visibility under clear conditions for navigation lights. The table at right shows these ranges according to the size of the boat. Note that, in addition to the information specified in this table, inconspicuous, partly submerged vessels or objects being towed should carry a white all-around light, visible at a distance of three miles.

Color Presentation

Color illustrations of required navigation-light groupings for various vessels follow on pages 33–40.

Rules 21–22: Colors and Areas of Visibility

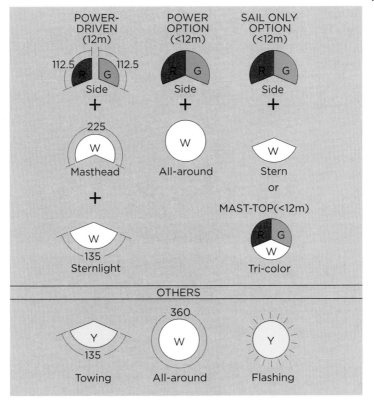

Type of light*	Vessel length in meters	Visibility in miles
MASTHEAD	under 12	2
	12–20	3
	20–50	5
	over 50	6
SIDE	under 12	1
	12–50	2
	over 50	3
STERN, TOWING, AND ALL-AROUND	under 50	2
	over 50	3

* Note also that inconspicuous, partly submerged vessels or objects being towed should carry a white all-around light, visible at a distance of three miles. *The Inland Rules also specify, for vessels of all lengths, a special flashing light, visible at a distance of two miles.*

Rule 23: Power-Driven Vessels Underway

RULE/VESSEL	GROUPS	SHAPES	VIEW FROM SIDE	BOW	STERN
INLAND (GREAT LAKES ONLY) **Rule 23(a)** Power-driven ≥ 50 m	Masthead Sidelights All-around for 2nd masthead + stern	None			
BOTH INTERNATIONAL AND INLAND **Rule 23(a)** Power-driven ≥ 50 m	2 Mastheads Sidelights Sternlight	None			
Rule 23(a) Power-driven <50 m	Masthead Sidelights Sternlight	None			
Rule 23(c) Power-driven optional <12 m	Sidelights All-around in lieu of masthead and stern	None			
INTERNATIONAL ONLY **Rule 23(c)(ii)** Power-driven <7 m & <7 kn max.	Sidelights if practical All-around	None			
BOTH INTERNATIONAL AND INLAND **Rule 23(a)** Submarine	2 Mastheads Sidelights Sternlight Flashing Yellow, 1/sec. for 3 sec., followed by 3 sec. off	None			
Rule 23(b) Hovercraft in displacement mode <50 m	Masthead Sidelights Sternlight	None			
Rule 23(b) Hovercraft non-displacement mode <50 m	Masthead Sidelights Sternlight Flashing Y	None			
INLAND ONLY **Rule 23(a)** Law Enforcement <50 m	Masthead Sidelights Sternlight Flashing Blue	None			

Rule 24: Vessels Towing and Pushing

RULE/VESSEL	GROUPS	SHAPES	VIEW FROM SIDE	BOW	STERN
BOTH INTERNATIONAL AND INLAND					
24(a)/Towing astern (Tow ≤ 200 m) If vessel ≥ 50m, add	2 vert. Mastheads Sidelights Sternlight Towlight Masthead aft	None			
24(a)/Towing astern (Tow > 200 m) If vessel ≥ 50 m, add	3 vert. Mastheads Sidelights Sternlight Towlight Masthead aft	◆			
24(b)/Composite (treated as single power vessel) If composite ≥ 50 m, add	Masthead Sidelights Sternlight Masthead aft	None			
24(c)/Pushing ahead or towing alongside (not composite) If vessel ≥ 50m, add	2 vert. Mastheads Sidelights Sternlight Masthead aft	None			
24(e)/Vessel/object being towed astern (other than 24(g)) (Tow ≤ 200 m)	Sidelights fwd Sternlight	None			
24(e)/Vessel/object being towed astern (other than 24(g)) (Tow > 200 m)	Sidelights fwd Sternlight	◆			
24(g)/Partly submerged 100 m long (<25 m wide) (≥ 25 m wide)	All-arounds fore & aft Add all-rounds on beam	◆			
Partly submerged >100 m long (<25 m wide) (≥ 25 m wide)	All-arounds fore & aft and every 100 m All-arounds fore & aft Add beam all-arounds @ 100 m	◆ ◆ aft fwd If tow >200 m			
INTERNATIONAL ONLY					
24(f)/Multiple vessels/objects pushed ahead	Sidelights fwd	None			
24(f)/Multiple vessels/objects towed alongside	Sidelights 2 Sternlights	None			
INLAND ONLY					
24(f)/Multiple vessels/objects pushed ahead	Sidelights fwd Special flashing	None			
24(f)/Multiple vessels/objects towed alongside	Sidelights 2 Sternlights Special flashing	None			
24(f)/Multiple vessels/objects towed alongside BOTH sides	Sidelights 2 Sternlights Special flashing	None			
INLAND Western Rivers except below Huey Long Bridge					
24(i)/Pushing ahead or towing alongside (not composite)	Sidelights 2 Towing lights NO Mastheads; No Sternlights	None			

Rule 25: Sailing Vessels Underway and Vessels Under Oars

RULE/VESSEL	GROUPS	SHAPES	VIEW FROM SIDE	BOW	STERN
BOTH INTERNATIONAL AND INLAND					
Rule 25(a) Sailing any length	Sidelights Sternlight	None			
Rule 25(b) Sailing <20 m option	Tri-color	None			
Rule 25(c) Sailing only optional any length	Sidelights Sternlight R/G all-around	None			
Rule 25(d)(i) Sailing or Rowing <7 m	Sidelights Sternlight	None			
Rule 25(d)(ii) Sailing or Rowing <7 m option	All-around or show only to prevent collision	None			
Rule 25(e) Motorsailing ≥ 50 m	2 Mastheads Sidelights Sternlight	▼			
Rule 25(e) Motorsailing <50 m	Masthead Sidelights Sternlight	▼			
Rule 25(e) Motorsailing <12 m	Masthead Sidelights Sternlight	▼ Optional under Inland Rules			

Rule 26: Fishing Vessels

RULE/VESSEL	GROUPS	SHAPES	VIEW FROM SIDE	BOW	STERN
BOTH INTERNATIONAL AND INLAND					
Rule 26(b) Trawling Making way ≥ 50 m	2 Mastheads Sidelights Sternlight G/W all-around				
Rule 26(b) Trawling Making way <50 m	Sidelights Sternlight G/W all-around				
Rule 26(b) Trawling, not making way	G/W all-around				
Rule 26(c) Fishing other than trawling, making way Any length	Sidelights Sternlight R/W all-around				
Rule 26(c) Fishing other than trawling, not making way Any length	R/W all-around				
Rule 26(c) Fishing other than trawling, making way Gear out >150 m	Sidelights Sternlight R/W all-around All-round	gear side			
Rule 26(c) Fishing other than trawling, not making way Gear out >150 m	Sidelights Sternlight R/W all-around All-round	gear side			

Rule 27: Vessels Not Under Command or Restricted in Their Ability to Maneuver

RULE/VESSEL	GROUPS	SHAPES	VIEW FROM SIDE	BOW	STERN
BOTH INTERNATIONAL AND INLAND					
Rule 27(a) Not Under Command Making way	Sidelights Sternlight R/R all-around				
Rule 27(a) Not Under Command Not making way	R/R all-around				
Rule 27(b) Restricted in Ability to Maneuver Making way <50 m	Masthead Sidelights Sternlight R/W/R all-around				
Rule 27(b) Restricted in Ability to Maneuver Making way ≥50 m	2 Mastheads Sidelights Sternlight R/W/R all-around				
Rule 27(b) Restricted in Ability to Maneuver Not making way	R/W/R all-around				
Rule 27(b) Restricted in Ability to Maneuver Anchored <50 m	R/W/R all-around W all-around				
Rule 27(b) Restricted in Ability to Maneuver Anchored 50 m	R/W/R all-around 2 W all-around				
Rule 27(d) Dredging or Underwater Operations Not making way	R/W/R all-around R/R all-rnd obstr. side G/G all-rnd clear side	obstr. side clear side			
Rule 27(e) Diving, but unable to display Underwater Operations lights	R/W/R all-around	Int'l Code Flag "A"			
Rule 27(f) Mine-clearing Making way ≥50 m	2 Mastheads Sidelights Sternlight G all-round				
Rule 27(f) Mine-clearing Making way <50 m	2 Mastheads Sidelights Sternlight G all-round				

Rule 28: Vessels Constrained by Their Draft (International Only)

RULE/VESSEL	GROUPS	SHAPES	VIEW FROM SIDE	BOW	STERN
INTERNATIONAL ONLY **Rule 28** Constrained by Draft Making way <50 m	Masthead Sidelights Sternlight R/R/R all-around	cylinder			
Rule 28 Constrained by Draft Making way If ≥50 m	Masthead Sidelights Sternlight R/R/R all-around 2nd Masthead	cylinder			

Rule 29: Pilot Vessels

RULE/VESSEL	GROUPS	SHAPES	VIEW FROM SIDE	BOW	STERN
BOTH INTERNATIONAL AND INLAND **Rule 29(a)** Pilot Vessel on Duty Underway	Sidelights Sternlight W/R all-around	Int'l Code Flag "H"			
Rule 29(a) Pilot Vessel on Duty Anchored	W/R all-around Anchor Light	Int'l Code Flag "H"			
Rule 29(b) Pilot Vessel off Duty Making way <50 m	Masthead Sidelights Sternlight	None			

Rule 30: Anchored Vessels and Vessels Aground

RULE/VESSEL	GROUPS	SHAPES	VIEW FROM SIDE	BOW	STERN
Rule 30(a) Anchored 50–100 m	2 W all-around	●			
Rule 30(b) Anchored ≥ 7m and <50 m	W all-around	●			
Rule 30(c) Anchored ≥ 100 m	2 W all-around All deck lights	●			
Rule 30(d) Aground ≥ 50 m	W all-around forward Lower W all-around aft R/R all-around (if practicable INLAND)	● ● ●			
Rule 30(d) Aground <50 m and ≥ 12 m	W all-around R/R all-around (if practicable INLAND)	● ● ●			
Rule 30(f) Aground <12 m	W all-around	●			

Rule 31: Seaplanes

RULE/VESSEL	GROUPS	SHAPES	VIEW FROM SIDE	BOW	STERN
Rule 31 Seaplane Underway	Masthead Sidelights Sternlight	None			

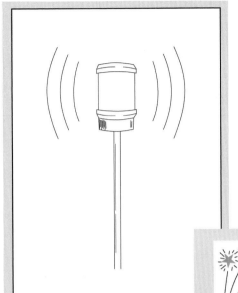

A high intensity white light flashing at regular intervals from 50 to 70 times per minute. (This is a distress signal used on Inland waters. See pages 97 and 112.)

RED STAR SHELLS	FOG HORN CONTINUOUS SOUNDING	FLAMES ON A VESSEL	GUN FIRED AT INTERVALS OF 1 MIN.
ORANGE BACKGROUND BLACK BALL AND SQUARE	SOS — SOS	"MAYDAY" BY RADIO	PARACHUTE RED FLARE
DYE MARKER (ANY COLOR)	CODE FLAGS NOVEMBER CHARLIE	SQUARE FLAG AND BALL	WAVE ARMS
RADIO-TELEGRAPH ALARM	RADIO-TELEPHONE ALARM	POSITION INDICATING RADIO BEACON	SMOKE

Distress signals (see pages 97 and 112).

VHF Radio

Most recreational boaters use the VHF radio to:

+ chitchat with their boating friends
+ arrange for fuel and docking
+ listen to marine weather forecasts
+ call for help when they break down

Strangely, few use it for its primary intended purpose—communication with other vessels regarding safe navigation. The Vessel Bridge-to-Bridge Radiotelephone Act requires certain vessels to monitor CH13 when underway within the three mile limit. These are:

+ power-driven vessels over twenty meters
+ inspected passenger vessels over 100 tons
+ towing vessels over twenty-six feet
+ dredges

In addition, the U.S. Coast Guard has established Security Broadcast Systems in most large coastal ports. In these systems, vessels required to monitor CH13 are also requested to report their movements fifteen minutes prior to getting underway, upon getting underway, and at certain check points in entering and leaving the port.

CH13 is thus your best source of information regarding the movements of large vessels in Inland waters. When you have a question regarding the intentions of another vessel—whether in a head-on, crossing, or overtaking situation—call the vessel first on CH13. If you get no response on CH13, try CH16.

A few ports, as well as traffic separation schemes and vessel traffic services, operate on channels other than CH13—usually CH11, CH12, or CH14. Consult the U.S. Coast Pilot, or call the nearest Coast Guard station on CH16 to obtain the channel for a specific area.

While the International Rules do not allow for the use of VHF radio in lieu of whistle signals, it has become common practice among large ships to exchange navigational information on CH16.

When contacting another vessel on VHF, keep in mind the area your signal will cover. CH13 is restricted to one watt, giving it an effective range of about five miles. The limit for CH16 is twenty-five watts, giving it a range of twenty or more miles. On CH13, you will be heard by every boat within eighty square miles; on CH16, you will be heard over at least one thousand square miles. Therefore, when attempting to contact an unknown vessel, be as specific as possible. Do not say, "I am calling the sailboat one mile on my port bow." The listener is not on your vessel, so he has no idea where your port bow is! Better to say, "I am calling a northerly-bound vessel. Captain, I am the fifty-foot white power vessel one mile on your starboard quarter." Now the listener knows exactly where to look to see if he is the one being hailed.

Part Two

International and Inland Rules

General

Rule 1: Application

WHAT IT SAYS

(a) These Rules shall apply to all vessels upon the high seas and in all waters connected therewith navigable by seagoing vessels. *These Rules apply to all vessels upon the inland waters of the United States, and to vessels of the United States on the Canadian waters of the Great Lakes to the extent that there is no conflict with Canadian law.*

(b) Nothing in these Rules shall interfere with the operation of special rules made by an appropriate authority for roadsteads, harbors, rivers, lakes or inland waterways connected with the high seas and navigable by seagoing vessels. Such special rules shall conform as closely as possible to these Rules.

(b) (i) These Rules constitute special rules made by an appropriate authority within the meaning of Rule 1 (b) of the International Regulations.

(ii) All vessels complying with the construction and equipment requirements of the International Regulations are considered to be in compliance with these Rules.

The italicized text indicates where the Inland Rules differ substantially from the COLREGS.

RULE 1

Application

(c) Nothing in these Rules shall interfere with the operation of any special rules made by the Government of any State *(the Secretary of the Navy)* with respect to additional station or signal lights, shapes or whistle signals for ships of war and vessels proceeding under convoy, with respect to additional station or signal lights or shapes for fishing vessels engaged in fishing as a fleet. These additional station or signal lights, shapes or whistle signals shall, so far as possible, be such that they cannot be mistaken for any light, shape or signal authorized elsewhere under these Rules.[1] *Notice of such special rules shall be published in the Federal Register and, after the effective date specified in such notice, they shall have effect as if they were a part of these Rules.[1]*

(d) Traffic separation schemes may be adopted by the Organization for the purpose of these Rules. *Traffic separation schemes may be established for the purposes of these Rules. Vessel traffic service regulations may be in effect in certain areas.*

(e) Whenever the Government *(Secretary)* concerned shall have determined that a vessel *(or class)* of special construction or purpose cannot comply fully with the provisions of any of these Rules with respect to the number, position, range or arc of visibility of lights or shapes, as well as to the disposition and characteristics of sound-signalling appliances, without interfering with the special function of the vessel, such vessel shall comply with such other provisions in regard to the number, position, range or arc of visibility of lights or shapes, as well as to the disposition and characteristics of sound signalling appliances, as her Government *(the Secretary)* shall have determined to be the closest possible compliance with these Rules in respect to that vessel. *The Secretary may issue a certificate of alternative compliance for a vessel or class of vessels specifying the closest possible compliance with these Rules. The Secretary of the Navy shall make these determinations and issue certificates of alternative compliance for vessels of the Navy.*

(f) *The Secretary may accept a certificate of alternative compliance issued by a contracting party to the International Regulations if he determines that the alternative compliance standards of the contracting party are substantially the same as those of the United States.*

---

[1] Submarines may display, as a distinctive means of identification, an intermittent flashing amber (yellow) beacon with a sequence of operation of one flash per second for three (3) seconds followed by a three (3) second off-period. Other special rules made by the Secretary of the Navy with respect to additional station and signal lights are found in Part 707 of Title 32, Code of Federal Regulations (32 CFR 707).

WHAT IT MEANS

The International Rules (COLREGS) apply to all of the oceans and bodies of water connected to them. In the U.S., the "special rules" consist of the United States Inland Rules, applicable to the Great Lakes, Western Rivers, waterways, and specific bays inside the magenta COLREGS Demarcation Line printed on charts.

RULE 1 Application

Some boaters think that the International Rules apply uniformly to any waters beyond three miles from land. The actual demarcation lines between the International and Inland Rules are listed in the back of the official *Navigation Rules: International—Inland*. There you will find that, with the exception of Casco Bay, the entire Coast of Maine, including its numerous deep bays, is subject to the International Rules. Similarly, Puget Sound on the West Coast falls under the International Rules. Study the demarcation lines in your area so that you will always know which rules apply.

Boats fishing as a fleet and warships may employ unique lights, shapes, and sound signals, as long as they cannot be confused with ones specified in the International Rules. Annex 2 of both the International and the Inland Rules, specifies the unique lights for trawlers and purse seiners fishing in close proximity. For example, purse seiners may show two yellow lights in a vertical line, flashing alternately every second, with equal on-off periods.

Traffic separation schemes are found in busy areas such as approaches to major harbors. They consist of one or more parallel pairs of inbound and outbound traffic lanes, each pair separated by a separation line or zone. The lanes and their termination points are clearly marked in magenta (red) on NOAA charts.

Boats of unusual construction or purpose may have noncomplying lights and sound-signals, as long as they do comply as closely as possible to the specifications in the rules. A submarine, for example, may have a forward steaming light lower than its sidelights, because it has no forward mast on which to mount the light.

Rule 2: Responsibility

WHAT IT SAYS

(a) Nothing in these Rules shall exonerate any vessel, or the owner, master or crew thereof, from the consequences of any neglect to comply with these Rules or of the neglect of any precaution which may be required by the ordinary practice of seamen, or by the special circumstances of the case.

(b) In construing and complying with these Rules due regard shall be had to all dangers of navigation and collision and to any special circumstances, including the limitations of the vessels involved, which may make a departure from these Rules necessary to avoid immediate danger.

RULE 2 Responsibility

WHAT IT MEANS

Rule 2 is the most important of the Rules. It charges that, no matter what happens, the person in charge of the vessel must do everything possible to avoid collision. In avoiding collision, you must consider your own vessel's maneuvering characteristics, the maneuvering characteristics of the other vessel, and any other hazards to navigation that may affect your decisions.

Rule 2 also says that you are allowed, and in some instances expected, to break the Rules when danger of collision is immediate. Departure from the Rules might be required, for example, by shallow water, a ledge or other obstruction, or the presence of other vessels.

In general, the Rules are designed to avoid collision between two vessels, not three or more. In a situation involving many vessels in a small area, you are forced to substitute common sense and good manners for the Rules. Rule 2 gives you permission.

In summary, Rule 2 removes any argument that a participant in a collision is without fault.

Rule 3: General Definitions

WHAT IT SAYS

For the purpose of these Rules (and this Act), except where the context otherwise requires:

(a) The word "Vessel" includes every description of water craft, including nondisplacement craft, WIG craft and seaplanes, used or capable of being used as a means of transportation on water.

(b) The term "Power-driven vessel" means any vessel propelled by machinery.

(c) The term "Sailing vessel" means any vessel under sail provided that propelling machinery, if fitted, is not being used.

(d) The term "Vessel engaged in fishing" means any vessel fishing with nets, lines, trawls or other fishing apparatus which restrict maneuverability, but does not include a vessel fishing with trolling lines or other fishing apparatus which do not restrict maneuverability.

(e) The word "Seaplane" includes any aircraft designed to maneuver on the water.

(f) The term "Vessel not under command" means a vessel which through some exceptional circumstance is unable to maneuver as required by these Rules and is therefore unable to keep out of the way of another vessel.

(g) The term "Vessel restricted in her ability to maneuver" means a vessel which from the nature of her work is restricted in her ability to maneuver as required by these Rules and is therefore unable to keep out of the way of another vessel. The term "Vessels restricted in their ability to maneuver" shall include but not be limited to:

(i) a vessel engaged in laying, servicing or picking up a navigation mark, submarine cable or pipeline;

(ii) a vessel engaged in dredging, surveying or underwater operations;

(iii) a vessel engaged in replenishment or transferring persons, provisions or cargo while underway;

(iv) a vessel engaged in the launching or recovery of aircraft;

(v) a vessel engaged in mine clearance operations;

(vi) a vessel engaged in a towing operation such as severely restricts the towing vessel and her tow in their ability to deviate from their course.

(h) The term "Vessel constrained by her draft" means a power-driven vessel which, because of her draft in relation to the available depth and width of navigable water is severely restricted in her ability to deviate from the course she is following.

Note that there is no mention of a "Vessel constrained by her draft" anywhere in the Inland Rules.

(i) The word "underway" means that a vessel is not at anchor, or made fast to the shore, or aground.

(j) The words "length" and "breadth" of a vessel mean her length overall and greatest breadth.

(k) Vessels shall be deemed to be in sight of one another only when one can be observed visually from the other.

(l) The term "restricted visibility" means any condition in which visibility is restricted by fog, mist, falling snow, heavy rainstorms, sandstorms or any other similar causes.

(m) The term "Wing-in-Ground (WIG) craft" means a multimodal craft which, in its main operational mode, flies in close proximity to the surface by utilizing surface-effect action.

(l) "Western Rivers" means the Mississippi River, its tributaries, South Pass, and Southwest Pass, to the navigational demarcation lines dividing the high seas from harbors, rivers, and other inland waters of the United States, and the Port Allen-Morgan City Alternate Route, and that part of the Atchafalaya River above its junction with the Port Allen-Morgan City Alternate Route including the Old River and the Red River;

(m) "Great Lakes" means the Great Lakes and their connecting and tributary waters including the Calumet River as far as the Thomas J. O'Brien Lock and Controlling Works (between mile 326 and 327), the Chicago River as far as the east side of the Ashland Avenue Bridge (between mile 321 and 322), and the Saint Lawrence River as far east as the lower exit of Saint Lambert Lock;

(n) "Secretary" means the Secretary of the department in which the Coast Guard is operating;

(o) "Inland Waters" means the navigable waters of the United States shoreward of the navigational demarcation lines dividing the high seas from harbors, rivers, and other inland waters of the United States and the waters of the Great Lakes on the United States side of the International Boundary;

(p) "Inland Rules" or "Rules" mean the Inland Navigational Rules and the annexes thereto, which govern the conduct of vessels and specify the lights, shapes, and sound signals that apply on inland waters; and

(q) "International Regulations" means the International Regulations for Preventing Collisions at Sea, 1972, including annexes currently in force for the United States.

WHAT IT MEANS
Definitions

Vessel: Anything capable of being used for transport on water. A bathtub, a log, even Herbie "the Lovebug," can all be vessels.

Power-driven vessel: Any vessel using an engine for propulsion.

Sailing vessel: Sailboat under sail, not using an engine for propulsion. With engine engaged it becomes, by definition, a "power-driven vessel."

Vessel engaged in fishing: Boat using fishing equipment that limits its maneuverability (nets, trawls, etc.). A sport-fishing, angling, or trolling boat is not a "vessel engaged in fishing" for the purposes of the Rules. A lobster or crab boat might be when it is hauling or setting traps. The key issue is the degree to which the fishing apparatus limits maneuverability. If you are sport fishing, don't take a chance.

Vessel not under command: Not "without a person in command," but rather a vessel that, due to accident, breakdown, or other circumstance, is unable to alter course or speed in order to avoid collision. Examples include boats whose engines or steering mechanisms have broken, boats dragging anchor, or becalmed sailboats with no auxiliary engine.

Vessel restricted in her ability to maneuver: Activities that specifically restrict ability to maneuver include: buoy tending, laying cable or pipe, dredging, surveying, diving, transferring materials underway, launching or recovering aircraft, minesweeping, and towing. The terminology, "vessel engaged in a towing operation such as severely restricts the towing vessel and her tow in their ability to deviate from their course," raises the question of the definition of the word "severely." Courtesy and caution dictate that you include any boat involved in towing.

Vessel constrained by her draft: Vessels having especially deep draft relative to the depth of water are allowed to claim special status under the International Rules. *There is no mention of a "vessel constrained by her draft" anywhere in the Inland Rules, no doubt because in inland waters, every boat would qualify.*

Underway: Not necessarily making way (moving relative to the water), but simply not anchored, grounded, or otherwise attached to shore. A "vessel at anchor" is one whose anchor is on the bottom and holding. A vessel dragging her anchor has at times been judged underway, at other times a "vessel not under command."

Length and breadth: Maximum or overall length, and maximum width.

Steering and Sailing Rules

SECTION 1 CONDUCT OF VESSELS IN ANY CONDITION OF VISIBILITY

Rule 4: Application

WHAT IT SAYS

Rules in this Section apply to any condition of visibility.

Rule 5: Lookout

WHAT IT SAYS

Every vessel shall at all times maintain a proper lookout by sight and hearing as well as by all available means appropriate in the prevailing circumstances and conditions so as to make a full appraisal of the situation and of the risk of collision.

RULES

4–5

Application/ Lookout

WHAT THEY MEAN

In over half of all marine accident hearings, both vessels involved in collision have been charged with failure to maintain an effective lookout.

In the case of the freighter *TFL Express,* which ran down the single-handed sailboat, *Granholm* (see page 15), the court assigned equal blame, saying, "The obligation to maintain a proper lookout falls upon great vessels and small alike."

In the case of the bulk carrier *Sealnes* running down the dive-tender *Mr. Fission* (see page 24), the *Sealnes* essentially relied on Vancouver vessel traffic services to maintain the lookout for them. The skipper of *Mr. Fission,* acting as owner, captain, and sidewalk superintendent of engine repairs, certainly failed to "at all times maintain a proper lookout."

It has been ruled that requiring a single individual to steer, navigate, and keep the lookout all at the same time is improper. The intent of the law is that the lookout devote his or her entire attention to the job of looking for other boats.

Further, it has been ruled that, considering limited visibility in fog and engine noise, a "proper lookout by sight and hearing" for any but the smallest of boats is one stationed at

The italicized text indicates where the Inland Rules differ substantially from the COLREGS.

RULES

4–5

**Application/
Lookout**

the bow, not at the helm. Communication between the helm and the lookout can be by intercom, or handheld VHF, if necessary.

What about a single-hander who inevitably must get some sleep? The court has ruled that failure of a single-hander to maintain a proper—i.e., constant—lookout, in spite of the need to sleep, is irresponsible in the sense of Rule 2. In other words, long, single-handed passages are themselves irresponsible.

"All available means" includes not only eyeballs and ears, but binoculars, radar, and VHF radio, as well. Obviously, radar should be used in fog, rain, and snow. But it should also be used at night, due to the possibility of unlit objects or vessels in your path. It has even been ruled that radar should be employed in clear daylight conditions, because of its unparalleled ability to measure range and bearing to targets.

Radar supplements, but does not replace, a visual lookout. Small wooden and fiberglass boats may be undetectable by radar beyond a fraction of a mile. With the radar on a long-range setting, close targets can be lost in the clutter. On the other hand, setting the radar to a short range may show close targets, but not potentially dangerous and fast-moving targets beyond the range, and it doesn't allow a sense of the overall traffic situation.

Vessels of 300 tons, passenger vessels of 100 tons, tow boats of twenty-six feet, and dredges working in or near channels are all required to communicate on VHF Channel 13. Vessels using traffic separation schemes and vessel traffic services also use designated VHF channels. Find out what these channels are, either by calling the Coast Guard or by consulting a Coast Pilot, and monitor them when in their areas.

Rule 6: Safe Speed

WHAT IT SAYS

Every vessel shall at all times proceed at a safe speed so that she can take proper and effective action to avoid collision and be stopped within a distance appropriate to the prevailing circumstances and conditions. In determining a safe speed the following factors shall be among those taken into account:

RULE 6

Safe Speed

(a) By all vessels:

    (i) the state of visibility;

    (ii) the traffic density including concentrations of fishing vessels or any other vessels;

    (iii) the maneuverability of the vessel with special reference to stopping distance and turning ability in the prevailing conditions;

    (iv) at night the presence of background light such as from shore lights or from back scatter of her own lights;

    (v) the state of wind, sea and current, and the proximity of navigational hazards;

    (vi) the draft in relation to the available depth of water.

(b) Additionally, by vessels with operational radar:

    (i) the characteristics, efficiency and limitations of the radar equipment;

    (ii) any constraints imposed by the radar range scale in use;

    (iii) the effect on radar detection of the sea state, weather and other sources of interference;

    (iv) the possibility that small vessels, ice and other floating objects may not be detected by radar at an adequate range;

    (v) the number, location and movement of vessels detected by radar;

    (vi) the more exact assessment of the visibility that may be possible when radar is used to determine the range of vessels or other objects in the vicinity.

RULE

6

Safe Speed

WHAT IT MEANS

Like automobiles, boats are required to limit their speed in order to be able to avoid collision. Factors determining safe speed include:

+ visibility conditions
+ background lights
+ traffic intensity
+ maneuverability
+ wind and current
+ navigational hazards
+ depth of water
+ the limitations of radar

How do you define "safe speed"? More than once, courts have applied as a rule of thumb "that speed which would allow stopping within half the range of visibility." Even this definition fails, however, when the hazards are below the surface. The atmospheric "visibility" was excellent on the night the *Titanic* struck the iceberg.

Note that the Rules do not define safe speed in so many words. Instead, the Rules tell you to constantly evaluate prevailing circumstances and conditions. Safe speed well outside a fog bank might be ten knots; safe speed within the fog might be only two knots; safe speed as you approach the fog bank would also be just a few knots, since you don't know what is headed toward you from inside it.

Rule 6 lists factors to be taken into account. The phrase "among those" means that the list is not to be considered complete. There is no way to predict what other special circumstances the prudent mariner should take into account in judging the safe speed for his/her boat.

Rule 6 also lists a number of additional factors to be considered by boats having radar. This list is likewise incomplete. Obviously, radar is an aid that tends to increase safe speed. Due to the limitations of radar and the limited reflectivity of some targets, however, it would be foolish to equate safe speed using radar to safe speed with unlimited visibility.

Mast-mounted radars on sailboats suffer from blind sectors of a few degrees. A wise precaution for the sailor is to periodically alter course five–ten degrees for a few sweeps of the radar, in order to see what's lurking or coming up in the blind sector.

The limitations of radar ranges were mentioned previously under Rule 5, Lookout. Good seamanship would include changing the range of the radar periodically in order to keep track of both the long-range situation and the weaker, close-in targets.

Both waves and precipitation return radar echoes. Since these are not of interest, they are considered to be noise or clutter. Radar sets are equipped with "clutter" controls to reduce (sea) wave and rain echoes, and should be used to produce the best discrimination under the circumstances. Clutter is reduced, however, by simply reducing overall sensitivity within a certain range, and should thus be taken into account when judging safe speed.

Safe speed is not necessarily zero speed. A boat dead in the water has no steerage and, therefore, no ability to change course to avoid collision. In particular, Rule 19(e) states that, under conditions of restricted visibility, a vessel that hears another vessel forward of her beam "shall reduce her speed to the minimum at which she can be kept on her course," i.e., to bare steerageway and "if necessary, take all her way off."

In spite of the fact that courts have repeatedly ruled "safe speed" to mean a speed that would allow a vessel to stop in one-half of its range of visibility, commercial vessels routinely operate at nearly top speed in conditions where they can barely see their own bows. The reasons are numerous: the pressure to maintain schedules; the illusion that radar is an infallible device; and a false sense of confidence that increases with each uneventful passage through fog.

The potential consequences of breaking Rule 6 are unimaginable. After losing the *Andrea Doria,* while operating at full speed in fog, her captain was heard to moan, "When I was a boy, and all my life, I loved the sea; now I hate it."

RULE

6

Safe Speed

Rule 7: Risk of Collision

WHAT IT SAYS

(a) Every vessel shall use all available means appropriate to the prevailing circumstances and conditions to determine if risk of collision exists. If there is any doubt such risk shall be deemed to exist.

(b) Proper use shall be made of radar equipment if fitted and operational, including long-range scanning to obtain early warning of risk of collision and radar plotting or equivalent systematic observation of detected objects.

(c) Assumptions shall not be made on the basis of scanty information, especially scanty radar information.

(d) In determining if risk of collision exists the following considerations shall be among those taken into account:

(i) such risk shall be deemed to exist if the compass heading of an approaching vessel does not appreciably change;

(ii) such risk may sometimes exist even when an appreciable bearing change is evident, particularly when approaching a very large vessel or a tow or when approaching a vessel at close range.

RULE

7

Risk of Collision

WHAT IT MEANS

You must use all available means to determine if collision with another boat is possible (not "likely," but "possible"). Collision is possible if the compass bearing (or relative bearing at steady course and speed) remains constant. If there is any doubt, you must assume collision is possible and act well in advance!

"All available means" to assess the risk of collision obviously includes the taking and plotting of compass bearings in clear visibility and the use of radar to track bearings in conditions of limited visibility. Consider- ing the ease of tracking relative bearings on even the least expensive small-boat radar, it is safe to assume that the use of radar under clear conditions would also be expected.

The warning "assumptions shall not be made on the basis of scanty information" relates mostly to the difficulty of taking accurate bearings. At long range, bearing errors of several degrees could produce opposing predictions of crossing ahead or crossing behind. If a boat is pitching or rolling, compass bearings can easily be five or more degrees in error.

Relative bearing (bearing relative to your boat's heading) is often used instead of compass bearing when using radar. Relative bearings are valid only if both heading and speed of the boat taking the bearing are constant, however. Similarly,

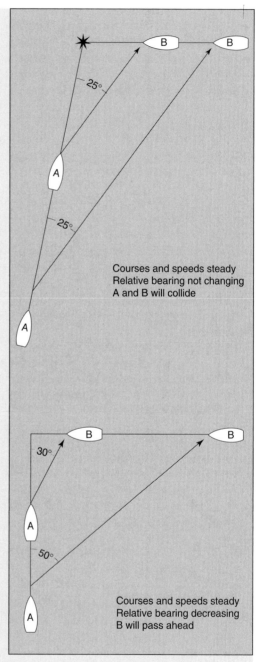

Courses and speeds steady
Relative bearing not changing
A and B will collide

Courses and speeds steady
Relative bearing decreasing
B will pass ahead

relative bearings taken by lining a target up against parts of your own boat (such as a stanchion) are only valid with constant speed and heading and a constant position of your eye!

You can use VHF radio to clarify another boat's intentions. But VHF has its limitations, chiefly the difficulty of determining the name of the boat you want to contact. A call to "the boat off Snug Harbor proceeding north," could raise several responses. To assume you have reached the intended boat might prove very dangerous. Better to state, "calling the trawler off Snug Harbor proceeding north. I am the overtaking white forty-foot sailboat one-half mile off your starboard quarter."

Never assume that a boat whose course seems unthreatening won't suddenly change it, thereby presenting a risk of collision. This is especially true at night and in fog, when the other boat might not even be aware of you. Assessing risk of collision is a full-time job. As you can see from the story on pages 17-18, the *Andrea Doria* ignored nearly every part of Rule 7:

(a) She failed to establish the identity and nature of the target first observed at seventeen miles, and, though there was certainly doubt as to whether risk of collision existed, she failed to assume its existence.

(b) Although she had a very accurate radar device, she failed to plot the course of the target in order to determine risk of collision.

(c) She assumed the other vessel to be a fishing vessel (and, therefore, assumed the vessel to be small and slow).

RULE

7

Risk of Collision

Rule 8: Action to Avoid Collision

WHAT IT SAYS

(a) Any action taken to avoid collision shall be taken in accordance with the Rules of this Part and shall, if the circumstances of the case admit, be positive, made in ample time and with due regard to the observance of good seamanship.

(b) Any alteration of course and/or speed to avoid collision shall, if the circumstances of the case admit, be large enough to be readily apparent to another vessel observing visually or by radar; a succession of small alterations of course and/or speed should be avoided.

(c) If there is sufficient sea room, alteration of course alone may be the most effective action to avoid a close-quarters situation provided that it is made in good time, is substantial and does not result in another close-quarters situation.

(d) Action taken to avoid collision with another vessel shall be such as to result in passing at a safe distance. The effectiveness of the action shall be carefully checked until the other vessel is finally past and clear.

RULE

8

Action to Avoid Collision

RULE

8

Action to Avoid Collision

(e) If necessary to avoid collision or allow more time to assess the situation, a vessel shall slacken her speed or take all way off by stopping or reversing her means of propulsion.

(f) (i) A vessel which, by any of these rules, is required not to impede the passage or safe passage of another vessel shall, when required by the circumstances of the case, take early action to allow sufficient sea room for the safe passage of the other vessel.

(ii) A vessel required not to impede the passage or safe passage of another vessel is not relieved of this obligation if approaching the other vessel so as to involve risk of collision and shall, when taking action, have full regard to the action which may be required by the rules of this part.

(iii) A vessel, the passage of which is not to be impeded remains fully obliged to comply with the rules of this part when the two vessels are approaching one another so as to involve risk of collision.

WHAT IT MEANS

Stress is placed on the fact that a give-way vessel must take significant and obvious action in ample time (before the stand-on vessel begins to question your intent). The alteration of course or speed must be large enough to be obvious to the other boat. At night, for example, the change of course should be large enough to show a different navigation light. Never make a series of small changes.

Given enough room, alterations to course are usually preferable to alterations in speed because course changes are more apparent from the other boat. Again, at night, the course change in a meeting or crossing situation should be large enough to display your opposite bow light; i.e., swing your bow past the stand-on boat.

On the other hand, a dramatic change in speed is acceptable if the stand-on boat is approaching you from your beam. In such a case, slowing down would be better than speeding up for several reasons:

(a) Rule 15 states, "When two power-driven vessels are crossing so as to involve risk of collision, the vessel which has the other on her own starboard shall keep out of the way and shall, if the circumstances of the case admit, avoid crossing ahead of the other vessel."

(b) Power boats usually travel at close to maximum speed anyway.

(c) If a collision did occur, damage would be less at low speed than at high speed.

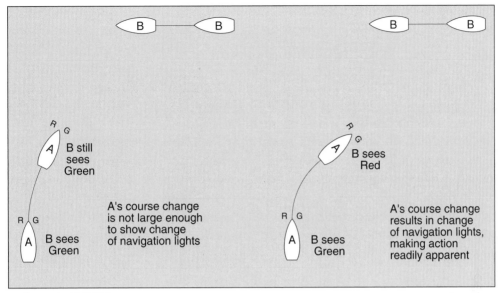

Action to Avoid Collision

Rule 9: Narrow Channels

WHAT IT SAYS

(a) *(i)* A vessel proceeding along the course of a narrow channel or fairway shall keep as near to the outer limit of the channel or fairway which lies on her starboard side as is safe and practicable.

(ii) Notwithstanding paragraph (a)(i) and Rule 14(a), a power-driven vessel operating in narrow channels or fairways on the Great Lakes, Western Rivers, or waters specified by the Secretary, and proceeding downbound with a following current shall have the right-of-way over an upbound vessel, shall propose the manner and place of passage, and shall initiate the maneuvering signals prescribed by rule 34(a)(i), as appropriate. The vessel proceeding upbound against the current shall hold as necessary to permit safe passing.

(b) A vessel of less than 20 meters in length or a sailing vessel shall not impede the passage of a vessel which can safely navigate only within a narrow channel or fairway.

(c) A vessel engaged in fishing shall not impede the passage of any other vessel navigating within a narrow channel or fairway.

(d) A vessel shall not cross a narrow channel or fairway if such crossing impedes the passage of a vessel which can safely navigate only within such channel or fairway. The latter vessel may *(shall)*

RULE
9

Narrow Channels

RULE 9

Narrow Channels

use the sound signal prescribed in Rule 34(d) if in doubt as to the intention of the crossing vessel.

(e) (i) In a narrow channel or fairway when overtaking can take place only if the vessel to be overtaken has to take action to permit safe passing*, the vessel intending to overtake shall indicate her intention by sounding the appropriate signal prescribed in Rule 34(c)(i). The vessel to be overtaken shall, if in agreement, sound the appropriate signal prescribed in Rule 34(c)(ii) and take steps to permit safe passing. If in doubt she may sound the signals prescribed in Rule 34(d).

(ii) This Rule does not relieve the overtaking vessel of her obligation under Rule 13.

(f) A vessel nearing a bend or an area of a narrow channel or fairway where other vessels may be obscured by an intervening obstruction shall navigate with particular alertness and caution and shall sound the appropriate signal prescribed in Rule 34(e).

(g) Any vessel shall, if the circumstances of the case admit, avoid anchoring in a narrow channel.

*Note that the Inland Rules require the overtaking vessel to give a sound signal regardless of whether action by the overtaken vessel is required.

WHAT IT MEANS

"Narrow channel" is not defined in the Rules. There are no limits to width, length, or depth of a narrow channel, except in relation to the boats involved. Generally, a channel may be considered narrow when, due to depth or distance between hazards, one or both boats are severely limited in room to maneuver. A channel marked by buoys may be considered a narrow channel by a deep draft boat, but not by a shallower draft boat that could navigate outside of the buoys.

Boats proceeding along narrow channels are required to stay, not just to the right of the centerline, but "as near to the outer limit of the channel or fairway that lies on her starboard side as is safe and practicable." Thus, smaller, shallower-draft boats should stay further to the right than larger, deeper-draft boats facilitating the passing of the larger, faster boats. You are also expected to remain on the starboard side, not just when encountering other boats but at all times.

Note that the Inland Rules differ on this point, stating that *"a downbound boat has the right-of-way over an upbound boat and should propose the manner of passing with the maneuvering signals in Rule 34."*

If a sailboat in a narrow channel cannot stay close to the starboard edge because she is tacking against the wind, she still must not impede a boat that can safely navigate only within the narrow channel or fairway.

Fishing is not prohibited in a narrow channel, but a fishing boat must get out of the

RULE

9

Narrow Channels

way of any other boat (not only a "vessel constrained by draft") that is using the channel.

You must not cross a narrow channel if your crossing will impede the passage of another boat that is constrained to the channel. Rule 9(d) does not prohibit crossing narrow channels at other times, nor does it override The Crossing Rule (Rule 15) for boats that are not constrained to the channel.

Under International Rules, when a boat being overtaken has to do anything but maintain course and speed to be safely passed, the boats must exchange the signals of Rule 34.

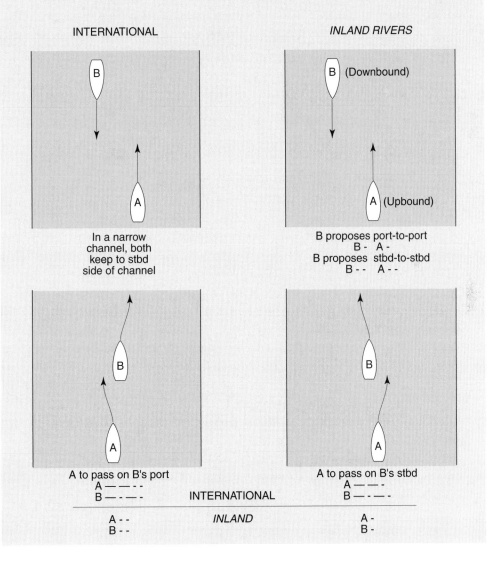

INTERNATIONAL

B

A

In a narrow channel, both keep to stbd side of channel

INLAND RIVERS

B (Downbound)

A (Upbound)

B proposes port-to-port
B -   A -
B proposes stbd-to-stbd
B - -   A - -

B

A

A to pass on B's port
A — — - -
B — - — -

INTERNATIONAL

INLAND

A - -
B - -

B

A

A to pass on B's stbd
A — — -
B — - — -

A -
B -

RULE

9

Narrow Channels

Under Inland Rules, however, a vessel intending to overtake another vessel in a narrow channel must initiate the signals of Rule 34, regardless of whether maneuvering is required of the overtaken vessel. When signals are given, the overtaking boat can only proceed after the overtaken boat has signaled agreement. If the overtaken boat does not agree, she must sound the danger signal. At this point, communication by VHF radio is in order before taking further action.

Boats approaching a bend or other blind area must sound one prolonged blast. Boats approaching in opposite directions and hearing the blast should respond in kind. Navigating "with particular alertness and caution" includes not cutting the corner when you can't see what is around the bend and allowing a vessel that is proceeding with the current to go first.

Rule 10: Traffic Separation Schemes

WHAT IT SAYS

RULE

10

Traffic Separation Schemes

(a) This Rule applies to traffic separation schemes adopted by the Organization and does not relieve any vessel of her obligation under any other rule.

(b) A vessel using a traffic separation scheme shall:

(i) proceed in the appropriate traffic lane in the general direction of traffic flow for that lane;

(ii) so far as practicable keep clear of a traffic separation line or separation zone;

(iii) normally join or leave a traffic lane at the termination of the lane, but when joining or leaving from either side shall do so at as small an angle to the general direction of traffic flow as practicable.

(c) A vessel shall, so far as practicable, avoid crossing traffic lanes but if obliged to do so shall cross on a heading as nearly as practicable at right angles to the general direction of traffic flow.

(d) (i) A vessel shall not use an inshore traffic zone when she can safely use the appropriate traffic lane within the adjacent traffic separation scheme. However, vessels of less than 20 meters in length, sailing vessels and vessels engaged in fishing may use the inshore traffic zone.

(ii) Notwithstanding subparagraph (d)(i), a vessel may use an inshore traffic zone when en route to or from a port, offshore installation or structure, pilot station or any other place situated within the inshore traffic zone, or to avoid immediate danger.

(e) A vessel other than a crossing vessel or a vessel joining or leaving a lane shall not normally enter a separation zone or cross a separation line except:

(i) in cases of emergency to avoid immediate danger;

(ii) to engage in fishing within a separation zone.

(f) A vessel navigating in areas near the terminations of traffic separation schemes shall do so with particular caution.

(g) A vessel shall so far as practicable avoid anchoring in a traffic separation scheme or in areas near its terminations.

(h) A vessel not using a traffic separation scheme shall avoid it by as wide a margin as is practicable.

(i) A vessel engaged in fishing shall not impede the passage of any vessel following a traffic lane.

(j) A vessel of less than 20 meters in length or a sailing vessel shall not impede the safe passage of a power-driven vessel following a traffic lane.

(k) A vessel restricted in her ability to maneuver when engaged in an operation for the maintenance of safety of navigation in a traffic separation scheme is exempted from complying with this Rule to the extent necessary to carry out the operation.

(l) A vessel restricted in her ability to maneuver when engaged in an operation for the laying, servicing or picking up of a submarine cable, within a traffic separation scheme, is exempted from complying with this Rule to the extent necessary to carry out the operation.

WHAT IT MEANS

Rule 10 applies only to traffic separation schemes in International Waters that have been formally adopted by the International Maritime Organization (IMO), plus the similar vessel traffic services in U.S. Inland Waters. Such schemes are marked in magenta on charts. The COLREGS apply within a TSS, just as elsewhere. When risk of collision arises within a TSS, all of the COLREGS rules, in addition to Rule 10, apply.

Who must use a TSS? Any vessel proceeding in the general direction of the TSS traffic lanes, except sailboats, motorboats less than twenty meters in length, and boats engaged in fishing, provided there is a separate inshore traffic zone available. Any vessel is permitted to transit an inshore traffic zone, however, to reach a location within it, or in order to avoid immediate danger.

Be especially careful near terminations because boats will be heading out in all directions.

Fishing is allowed both in traffic lanes and in the separation zone between lanes. However:

+ Boats fishing in a traffic lane must move in the general direction of traffic and must not impede the passage of any other boat using the lane.

RULE

10

Traffic Separation Schemes

+ Boats fishing in a separation zone may proceed in any direction but must not let their nets extend into a traffic zone and impede the passage of any other boat using the traffic lane.

When operating in the vicinity of a traffic separation scheme, find the VHF radio channel used by vessels transiting the scheme and monitor it, particularly in conditions of limited visibility.

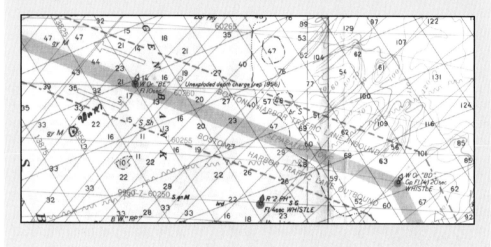

SECTION 2 CONDUCT OF VESSELS IN SIGHT OF ONE ANOTHER

Rule 11: Application

WHAT IT SAYS

RULE

11

Application

Rules in this section apply to vessels in sight of one another.

WHAT IT MEANS

Note that "in sight" means able to be observed by eye; it does not refer to the use of radar.

Rule 12: Sailing Vessels

WHAT IT SAYS

(a) When two sailing vessels are approaching one another, so as to involve risk of collision, one of them shall keep out of the way of the other as follows:

(i) when each has the wind on a different side, the vessel which has the wind on the port side shall keep out of the way of the other;

(ii) when both have the wind on the same side, the vessel which is to windward shall keep out of the way of the vessel which is to leeward;

(iii) if a vessel with the wind on the port side sees a vessel to windward and cannot determine with certainty whether the other vessel has the wind on the port or on the starboard side, she shall keep out of the way of the other.

(b) For the purposes of this Rule the windward side shall be deemed to be the side opposite to that on which the mainsail is carried or, in the case of a square-rigged vessel, the side opposite to that on which the largest fore-and-aft sail is carried.

RULE
12
Sailing Vessels

WHAT IT MEANS

A sailboat is a "sailing vessel" only when she is using her sails as her only source of propulsion. The common practice of motorsailing—using the engine to help the sails—renders a sailboat a "power-driven vessel" for the purposes of the Rules. Be aware that many novice sailboaters aren't aware of this distinction and may assume they are the stand-on vessel in an encounter with a motorboat.

The "tack" of a sailboat is not the side the wind is coming over, but the side opposite that on which the main sail is carried. Of course, the two are the same ninety-nine percent of the time, but the location of the main sail is more easily seen from another boat than is the direction of the wind. Note that in the case of a square-rigged ship, the tack is determined by the largest fore-and-aft sail.

Sailors must remember that Rules 13, 16, 17, and 18 also apply when risk of collision exists between two sailboats:

+ Rule 13 (Overtaking) overrules Rule 12 when one of the sailboats is overtaking the other from more than 22.5° abaft the beam.

+ Rules 16 (Action by Give-way Vessel) and 17 (Action by Stand-on Vessel) apply to two sailboats, just as to other types of vessels.

RULE
12
Sailing Vessels

✦ Rule 18 states that a sailboat must keep out of the way of another sailboat that is both sailing and fishing and any other boat that is not under command. Given the definition of fishing in the Rules (does not include angling or sport-trolling), it is unlikely that you will encounter a boat both sailing and fishing anywhere but in a third-world country.

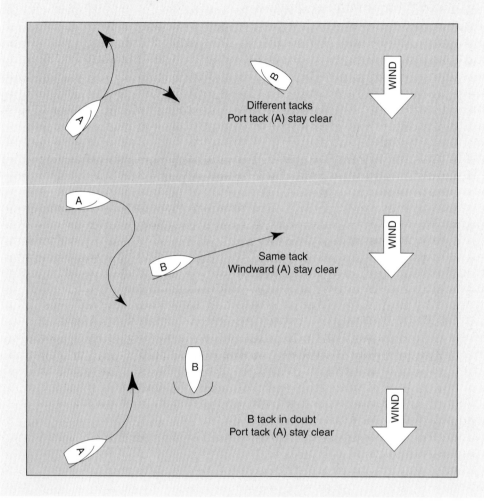

Rule 13: Overtaking

WHAT IT SAYS

(a) Notwithstanding anything contained in the Rules of Part B: Sections 1 and 2 *(Rules 4–18)*, any vessel overtaking any other shall keep out of the way of the vessel being overtaken.

(b) A vessel shall be deemed to be overtaking when coming up with another vessel from a direction more than 22.5 degrees abaft her beam, that is, in such a position with reference to the vessel she is overtaking, that at night she would be able to see only the sternlight of that vessel but neither of her sidelights.

(c) When a vessel is in any doubt as to whether she is overtaking another, she shall assume that this is the case and act accordingly.

(d) Any subsequent alteration of the bearing between the two vessels shall not make the overtaking vessel a crossing vessel within the meaning of these Rules or relieve her of the duty of keeping clear of the overtaken vessel until she is finally past and clear.

RULE
13
Overtaking

WHAT IT MEANS

Since an overtaken boat is likely to be slower and, thus, less able to get out of the way, an overtaking vessel must always give way.

If the other boat's sidelight is visible at the same time as its sternlight, then the situation is crossing, rather than overtaking.

During daylight, without benefit of the other boat's lights, it may be hard to tell whether you are overtaking, since the 22.5° aft-of-the-beam bearing is defined relative to the beam of the overtaken boat, not that of the overtaking boat. For this reason, Rule 13(c) states that, when there is any doubt, a vessel should assume she is overtaking.

At some time during the overtaking maneuver, the overtaking boat will obviously pull forward of the overtaking sector. For this reason, Rule 13(d) states that an overtaking boat continues to be the give-way boat until she is past and clear of the overtaken boat.

An interesting scenario: Boat 1 passes slower Boat 2, at a great distance, on Boat 2's starboard side. Boat 1 then turns, to cross Boat 2 from Boat 2's starboard side. Does Boat 1 have the right in the new crossing situation, or has she failed to keep out of the way until past and clear?

If such a case went to court, the key issue would probably be whether risk of collision had existed before Boat 1 turned to become a crossing boat. If the passing had taken place at such a distance that risk of collision had never existed, then Boat 1 would never have been an overtaking vessel and, thus, never charged with staying clear. In case of doubt, however,

RULE

13

Overtaking

the passing boat would be wise to keep out of the way and not push a questionable claim.

Just because an overtaking boat is burdened with keeping out of the way of an overtaken boat, Rule 13 does not give sailboats, boats of less than twenty meters in length, and fishing boats the right to impede the passage of an overtaking boat in a narrow channel or traffic lane. However, the overtaking boat must first obtain agreement from the overtaken boat and take whatever precautions she can to make the overtaking safe.

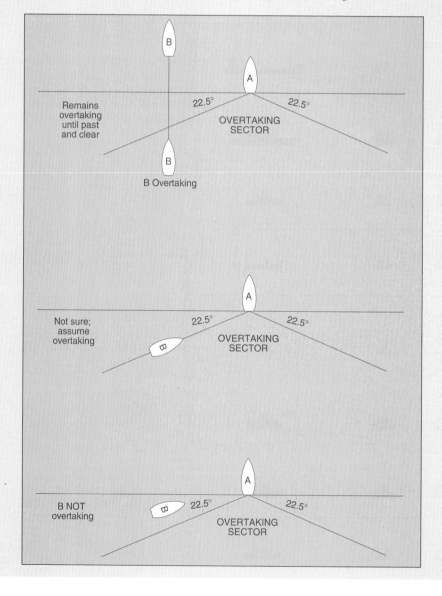

Rule 14: Head-on Situation

WHAT IT SAYS

(a) *(Unless otherwise agreed)* When two power-driven vessels are meeting on reciprocal or nearly reciprocal courses so as to involve risk of collision each shall alter her course to starboard so that each shall pass on the port side of the other.

(b) Such a situation shall be deemed to exist when a vessel sees the other ahead or nearly ahead and by night she could see the masthead lights of the other in a line or nearly in a line and/or both sidelights and by day she observes the corresponding aspect of the other vessel.

(c) When a vessel is in any doubt as to whether such a situation exists she shall assume that it does exist and act accordingly.

(d) *Notwithstanding paragraph (a) of this Rule, a power-driven vessel operating on the Great Lakes, Western Rivers, or waters specified by the Secretary, and proceeding downbound with a following current shall have the right-of-way over an upbound vessel, shall propose the manner of passage, and shall initiate the maneuvering signals prescribed by Rule 34 (a)(1), as appropriate.*

RULE
14
Head-On Situation

WHAT IT MEANS

Note that the rule applies only to powerboats, not to vessels that are sailing, fishing, restricted-in-ability-to-maneuver, or not-under-command.

Note also the phrase "so as to involve risk of collision." Although the rule states that boats meeting head-on should pass port-to-port, this does not mean that you can never pass starboard-to-starboard. Before a risk of collision exists, either boat can alter course so long as the course change requires no subsequent action by the other vessel.

Once risk of collision exists, or when the boats are within a half-mile of each other, U.S. Inland Rules state that the boats must indicate their maneuvers or intent to maneuver with the signals of Rule 34. They may agree to pass starboard-to-starboard, but they should have a good reason to do so.

It is increasingly common under Inland Rules for boats to signal their intentions via VHF radio, referring to port-to-port as "one whistle" and starboard-to-starboard as "two whistles." This may be acceptable between professional mariners but is very dangerous between weekend boaters, since some skippers don't understand the meanings and may be reluctant to admit it in front of their passengers. In the interest of safety, pass port-to-port whenever possible and indicate your intentions in those words.

A "reciprocal or nearly reciprocal course" is:

✦   when a boat sees another boat ahead or nearly ahead;
✦   when at night she sees the masthead lights of the other in a line or nearly in a line;
✦   when at night she sees both sidelights.

Of the three criteria, the third is the most precise because sidelights are designed to shine only one–three degrees to the opposite side of the centerline, so that when both lights are seen simultaneously, the two boats are theoretically within about two degrees of head-on. Allowing for yawing, if you see both sidelights simultaneously, either constantly or occasionally, then the boat is within about five degrees of head-on.

A fine distinction, which could become important in a strong cross current, is whether the rule truly means reciprocal courses (referring to the direction of motion) or reciprocal headings (referring to the direction in which the boat is pointed). Paragraph 14(a) indicates course, but paragraph 14(b) says that a reciprocal course shall be deemed to exist when both sidelights can be seen, indicating a reciprocal heading. Paragraph 14(c) resolves the conflict by stating that, in case of doubt, you are to assume that the situation is head-on.

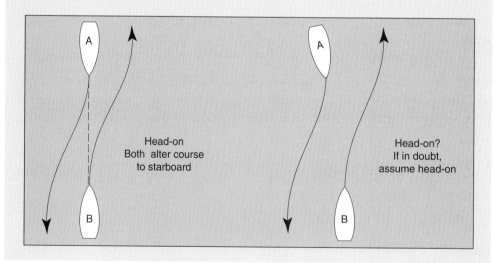

Rule 15: Crossing Situation

WHAT IT SAYS

(a) When two power-driven vessels are crossing so as to involve risk of collision, the vessel which has the other on her own starboard side shall keep out of the way and shall, if the circumstances of the case admit, avoid crossing ahead of the other vessel.

(b) Notwithstanding paragraph (a), on the Great Lakes, Western Rivers, or water specified by the Secretary, a vessel crossing a river shall keep out of the way of a power-driven vessel ascending or descending the river.

RULE

15

Crossing Situation

WHAT IT MEANS

Note that Rule 15 applies only:

- ✦ to two boats, not three or more;
- ✦ to power-driven boats (not to boats that are sailing, fishing, not under command, or restricted in their ability to maneuver);
- ✦ in crossing (not head-on or overtaking) situations;
- ✦ after risk of collision has been determined to exist.

Before risk of collision has been established, either boat is free to maneuver at will. Once risk of collision has been established, however, the boat with the other vessel approaching on her starboard side:

- ✦ becomes the give-way boat;
- ✦ must not cross ahead of the stand-on boat unless circumstances require it.

Remember that a boat approaching on your starboard side sees your green (go) light, while a boat approaching on your port side sees your red (stop) light.

Before crossing a narrow channel, remember Rule 9(d), "A vessel shall not cross a narrow channel or fairway if such crossing impedes the passage of a vessel which can safely navigate only within such channel or fairway."

Similarly, when you are in a traffic separation scheme, remember that Rule 10(j) states, "A vessel of less than 20 meters in length … shall not impede the safe passage of a power-driven vessel following a traffic lane."

When an ordinary power-driven boat meets a fishing or hampered boat, Rule 18, rather

RULE

15

Crossing Situation

than Rule 15, applies. Therefore, if your power boat is approached on its port side by a fishing or hampered boat, you must keep clear. You are not, however, forbidden to cross ahead of the stand-on boat, as you would be under Rule 15.

The rules governing a situation in which a power boat meets a boat constrained by her draft contain subtle distinctions. First, the boat constrained by her draft can only claim those special rights by displaying the proper signals. Provided the signals are displayed, then the ordinary power boat must "avoid impeding the safe passage of the vessel constrained by her draft" by taking action before risk of collision develops. However, once risk of collision has been established, a constrained-by-draft boat approaching on the port side of an ordinary power boat becomes the give-way boat under Rule 15.

A power boat underway, but not making way through the water, has no special rights. If she is stopped because she is either anchored or broken down (not under command), then she should display the proper anchored or not-under-command signals. If not, and if she is approached by another power boat from dead ahead to 22.5 degrees abaft her starboard beam, then she'd better get some way on and get out of the way!

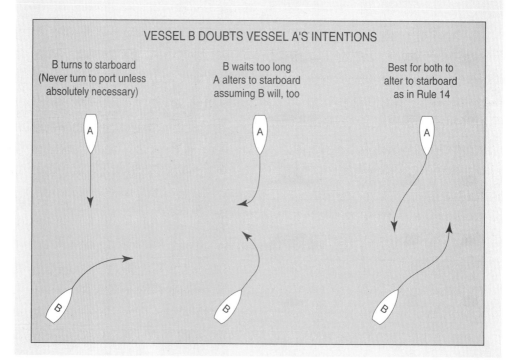

VESSEL B DOUBTS VESSEL A'S INTENTIONS

B turns to starboard
(Never turn to port unless
absolutely necessary)

B waits too long
A alters to starboard
assuming B will, too

Best for both to
alter to starboard
as in Rule 14

Rule 16: Action by Give-Way Vessel

WHAT IT SAYS

Every vessel that is directed to keep out of the way of another vessel shall, so far as possible, take early and substantial action to keep well clear.

WHAT IT MEANS

In essence, Rule 16 simply states that a give-way vessel must give way in the manner prescribed in Rule 8.

Rule 17: Action by Stand-On Vessel

WHAT IT SAYS

(a) (i) Where one of two vessels is to keep out of the way, the other shall keep her course and speed.

(ii) The latter vessel may, however, take action to avoid collision by her maneuver alone, as soon as it becomes apparent to her that the vessel required to keep out of the way is not taking appropriate action in compliance with these Rules.

(b) When, from any cause, the vessel required to keep her course and speed finds herself so close that collision cannot be avoided by the action of the give-way vessel alone, she shall take such action as will best aid to avoid collision.

(c) A power-driven vessel which takes action in a crossing situation in accordance with sub-paragraph (a)(ii) of this Rule to avoid collision with another power-driven vessel shall, if the circumstances of the case admit, not alter course to port for a vessel on her own port side.

(d) This Rule does not relieve the give-way vessel of her obligation to keep out of the way.

WHAT IT MEANS

Rule 17 applies only where risk of collision exists between two (not three or more) boats. In such a situation, the boat required to keep out of the way is the "give-way vessel" (Rule 16). Rule 17 covers the other boat, the "stand-on vessel."

The actions permitted/required of the stand-on vessel take place in four stages:

RULE

17

Action by Stand-On Vessel

1. Before risk of collision exists, either boat is free to maneuver at will.

2. Once risk of collision exists, except to avoid hazards, the stand-on boat must maintain course and speed.

3. If it becomes apparent to the stand-on boat that the give-way boat is not taking the appropriate (early and substantial) action to keep out of the way, then the stand-on boat is *permitted* to take action to avoid collision. If both boats are power-driven, however, the action must not be a turn to port for a give-way boat on her port. Any maneuver she makes must be accompanied by the appropriate maneuvering signal in Rule 34. If she chooses not to maneuver, then she should sound the danger signal (five short whistles) as a wake-up call to the unresponsive give-way boat. If the give-way vessel is readily identified either by name, characteristics, or location, then a call on VHF CH13 or 16 would be appropriate, in addition.

4. If the situation deteriorates to the point where collision can no longer be avoided by action of the give-way boat alone, the stand-on boat is *required* to take the best action it can to avoid collision. Again, the action should be accompanied by the appropriate sound signals. At this late stage, a turn to port is not absolutely prohibited. In fact, if it appears that the give-way boat is about to strike the stand-on boat aft, a hard turn to port might be the best maneuver to avoid collision.

The timing and nature of a stand-on boat's Stage 3 actions are critical. If she takes action too soon, she may find herself acting simultaneously with the give-way boat. To prevent escalation of the confusion, the stand-on boat should always:

+ turn to starboard;
+ accompany the maneuver with the appropriate signal so that the give-way boat understands her action.

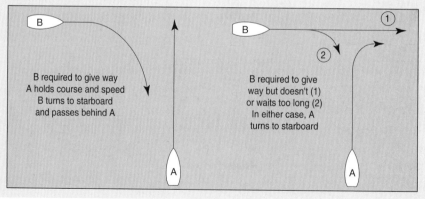

B required to give way
A holds course and speed
B turns to starboard
and passes behind A

B required to give
way but doesn't (1)
or waits too long (2)
In either case, A
turns to starboard

Rule 18: Responsibilities Between Vessels

WHAT IT SAYS

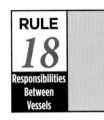

Except where Rules 9, 10, and 13 otherwise require:

(a) A power-driven vessel underway shall keep out of the way of:

    (i) a vessel not under command;

    (ii) a vessel restricted in her ability to maneuver;

    (iii) a vessel engaged in fishing; and

    (iv) a sailing vessel.

(b) A sailing vessel underway shall keep out of the way of:

    (i) a vessel not under command;

    (ii) a vessel restricted in her ability to maneuver; and

    (iii) a vessel engaged in fishing.

(c) A vessel engaged in fishing when underway shall, so far as possible, keep out of the way of:

    (i) a vessel not under command;

    (ii) a vessel restricted in her ability to maneuver.

(d) (i) A vessel other than a vessel not under command or a vessel restricted in her ability to maneuver shall, if the circumstances of the case admit, avoid impeding the safe passage of a vessel constrained by her draft, exhibiting the signals in Rule 28.

    (ii) A vessel constrained by her draft shall navigate with particular caution having full regard to her special condition.

Note that there is no mention of a "vessel constrained by her draft" anywhere in the Inland Rules.

(e) A seaplane on the water shall, in general, keep well clear of all vessels and avoid impeding their navigation. In circumstances, however, where risk of collision exists, she shall comply with the Rules of this Part.

(f) (i) A WIG craft shall, when taking off, landing and in flight near the surface, keep well clear of all other vessels and avoid impeding their navigations.

    (ii) A WIG craft operating on the water surface shall comply with the Rules of this Part as a power-driven vessel.

RULE

18

Responsibilities
Between
Vessels

WHAT IT MEANS

Rule 18 applies to all situations except for:

+ Narrow channels (Rule 9)
+ Traffic separation schemes (Rule 10)
+ Overtaking situations (Rule 13)

The rule establishes a "pecking order" between types of boats. Boats higher than you on the list are considered the "stand-on" vessel in a collision situation; vessels below you are the "give-way" vessel. The top two (vessel not under command and vessel restricted in ability to maneuver) share equal status, however. The list, in order of decreasing rights:

+ Vessel not under command, and vessel restricted in ability to maneuver
+ Vessel constrained by draft
+ Vessel engaged in fishing
+ Sailing vessel
+ Power-driven vessel
+ Seaplane

Example: A sailboat (powered by sail alone) must keep out of the way of vessels engaged in fishing, constrained by draft, restricted in ability to maneuver, and not under command (all of the vessel types above it in the list), but not ordinary power boats or seaplanes. To claim special status, a boat must display the appropriate lights or shapes. Therefore, a fishing boat not displaying fishing or trawling lights or shapes and a tug not displaying the lights or shapes for a vessel restricted in ability to maneuver are to be considered simply power-driven vessels. A sailboat while motorsailing, however, reverses this logic. By displaying a cone, apex down (required of all motorsailing vessels except those less than twelve meters under Inland Rules), it drops in status from sailing to power-driven.

Since the special privilege signals are often not spotted or identified (probably less than ten percent of all recreational boaters would be able to identify such signals), privileged boats should always be prepared to sound the danger signal (five short blasts).

Rule 19: Conduct of Vessels in Restricted Visibility

WHAT IT SAYS

(a) This Rule applies to vessels not in sight of one another when navigating in or near an area of restricted visibility.

(b) Every vessel shall proceed at a safe speed adapted to the prevailing circumstances and conditions of restricted visibility. A power-driven vessel shall have her engines ready for immediate maneuver.

(c) Every vessel shall have due regard to the prevailing circumstances and conditions of restricted visibility when complying with Rules of Section 1 of this Part (Rules 4 through 10).

(d) A vessel which detects by radar alone the presence of another vessel shall determine if a close-quarters situation is developing and/or risk of collision exists. If so, she shall take avoiding action in ample time, provided that when such action consists of an alteration of course, so far as possible the following shall be avoided:

> (i) an alteration of course to port for a vessel forward of the beam, other than for a vessel being overtaken; and

> (ii) an alteration of course toward a vessel abeam or abaft the beam.

(e) Except where it has been determined that a risk of collision does not exist, every vessel which hears apparently forward of her beam the fog signal of another vessel, or which cannot avoid a close-quarters situation with another vessel forward of her beam, shall reduce her speed to the minimum at which she can be kept on course. She shall if necessary take all her way off and, in any event, navigate with extreme caution until danger of collision is over.

RULE

19

Conduct of Vessels in Restricted Visibility

The italicized text indicates where the Inland Rules differ substantially from the COLREGS.

WHAT IT MEANS

Rule 19 applies only to boats, in or near restricted visibility, that can not see each other by eye. If the boats subsequently do see each other, Rules 11–18 take over.

The phrase "in or near an area of restricted visibility" is more important than one might think. Courts have found that a boat failing to slow to safe speed before entering an area of restricted visibility is just as liable as one speeding inside the area. The point is that a boat outside the area cannot see a boat inside the area and vice-versa. The visibility is no greater than if both were inside the area.

RULE 19

Conduct of Vessels in Restricted Visibility

Rule 19 repeats the injunction of Rule 6 to, at all times, proceed at a safe speed. This is a very hard rule to follow in fog, as the courts have repeatedly judged "safe speed" to be that which would allow stopping in one-half the distance of visibility. For any vessel in dense fog, this translates into stopping altogether!

Rule 19(b) also instructs a power boat to keep her "engines ready for immediate maneuver." She would, however, probably be excused for shutting her engines down briefly in order to better listen for sound signals. "Ready for immediate maneuver" presumably includes the steering mechanism. If so, a boat in limited visibility should be on manual steering—not autopilot—and the helmsman should have one hand on the throttle.

The phrase, "so far as possible," is inserted in paragraph 19(d) to allow for the possibility of limited sea room due to navigational hazards or the near presence of other boats.

Paragraph 19(e) refers to "except where it has been determined that a risk of collision does not exist." The only defensible, yet still risky, method of making such a determination in fog is through a series of radar bearings. If you don't have radar, or are not proficient in taking and plotting radar bearings, you obviously cannot say that you have determined there to be no risk.

Unless you have determined there is no risk of collision, when you hear a fog signal forward of your beam or otherwise find yourself in close quarters with another boat forward of your beam, you must reduce your speed to bare steerageway, or even stop dead in the water. Also, while Rule 35 specifies the maximum interval between fog signals, it does not prevent blowing your horn more often.

Finally, not mentioned in the Rules, but prudent behavior: If you hear a boat approaching from forward of your beam, you might want to take all way off. First, however, turn to face the other boat head-on, for two reasons:

+ To present a smaller target.
+ To take a possible blow at your boat's least vulnerable point—her bow.

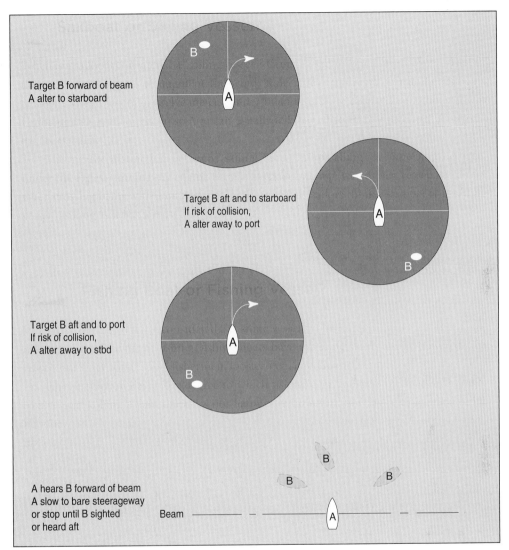

Target B forward of beam
A alter to starboard

Target B aft and to starboard
If risk of collision,
A alter away to port

Target B aft and to port
If risk of collision,
A alter away to stbd

A hears B forward of beam
A slow to bare steerageway
or stop until B sighted
or heard aft

Beam

Lights and Shapes

Rule 20: Application

WHAT IT SAYS

(a) Rules in this Part shall be complied with in all weathers.

(b) The Rules concerning lights shall be complied with from sunset to sunrise, and during such times no other lights shall be exhibited, except such lights as cannot be mistaken for the lights specified in these Rules or do not impair their visibility or distinctive character, or interfere with the keeping of a proper lookout.

(c) The lights prescribed by these Rules shall, if carried, also be exhibited from sunrise to sunset in restricted visibility and may be exhibited in all other circumstances when it is deemed necessary.

(d) The Rules concerning shapes shall be complied with by day.

(e) The lights and shapes specified in these Rules shall comply with the provisions of Annex I of these Regulations.

The italicized text indicates where the Inland Rules differ substantially from the COLREGS.

WHAT IT MEANS

Lights must be displayed at night (sunset to sunrise) and during the day in restricted visibility. Shapes must be displayed from sunrise to sunset, regardless of visibility. Lights that could be confused with the official lights or affect the lookout are prohibited.

Rule 21: Definitions

WHAT IT SAYS

RULE

21

Definitions

(a) "Masthead light" means a white light placed over the fore and aft centerline of the vessel showing an unbroken light over an arc of the horizon of 225 degrees and so fixed as to show the light from right ahead to 22.5 degrees abaft the beam on either side of the vessel (*except that on a vessel of less than 12 meters in length the masthead light shall be placed as nearly as practicable to the fore and aft centerline of the vessel*).

(b) "Sidelights" mean a green light on the starboard side and a red light on the port side each showing an unbroken light over an arc of the horizon of 112.5 degrees and so fixed as to show the light from right ahead to 22.5 degrees abaft the beam on its respective side. In a vessel of less than 20 meters in length the sidelights may be combined in one lantern carried on the fore and aft centerline of the vessel (*except that on a vessel of less than 12 meters in length the sidelights when combined in one lantern shall be placed as nearly as practicable to the fore and aft centerline of the vessel*).

(c) "Sternlight" means a white light placed as nearly as practicable at the stern showing an unbroken light over an arc of the horizon of 135 degrees and so fixed as to show the light 67.5 degrees from right aft on each side of the vessel.

(d) "Towing light" means a yellow light having the same characteristics as the "sternlight" defined in paragraph (c) of this Rule.

(e) "All-round light" means a light showing an unbroken light over an arc of the horizon of 360 degrees.

(f) "Flashing light" means a light flashing at regular intervals at a frequency of 120 flashes or more per minute.

(g) *"Special flashing light"means a yellow light flashing at regular intervals at a frequency of 50 to 70 flashes per minute, placed as far forward and as nearly as practicable on the fore and aft center-line of the tow and showing an unbroken light over an arc of the horizon of not less than 180 degrees nor more than 225 degrees and so fixed as to show the light from right ahead to abeam and no more than 22.5 degrees abaft the beam on either side of the vessel.*

WHAT IT MEANS

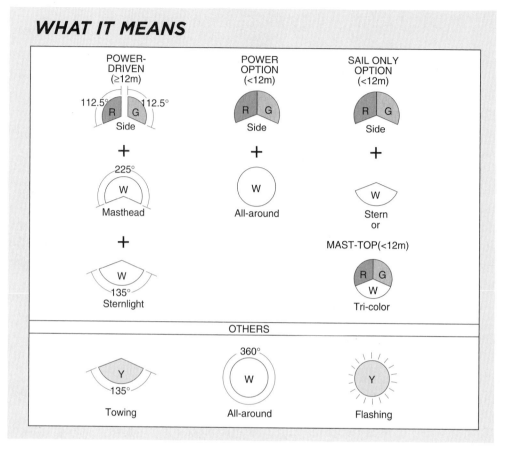

Rule 22: Visibility of Lights

WHAT IT SAYS

The lights prescribed in these Rules shall have an intensity as specified in Section 8 of Annex I to these Rules, so as to be visible at the following minimum ranges:

(a) In a vessel of 50 meters or more in length:

    —a masthead light, 6 miles;

    —a sidelight, 3 miles;

    —a sternlight, 3 miles;

    —a towing light, 3 miles;

    —a white, red, green or yellow all-round light, 3 miles; and

    —*a special flashing light, 2 miles.*

(b) In a vessel of 12 meters or more in length but less than 50 meters in length:
  —a masthead light, 5 miles; except that where the length of the vessel is less than 20 meters, 3 miles;
  —a sidelight, 2 miles;
  —a sternlight, 2 miles;
  —a towing light, 2 miles;
  —a white, red, green or yellow all-round light, 2 miles; and
  —*a special flashing light, 2 miles.*
(c) In a vessel of less than 12 meters in length:
  —a masthead light, 2 miles;
  —a sidelight, 1 mile;
  —a sternlight, 2 miles;
  —a towing light, 2 miles;
  —a white, red, green or yellow all-round light, 2 miles; and
  —*a special flashing light, 2 miles.*
(d) In an inconspicuous, partly submerged vessel or object being towed:
  —a white all-round light, 3 miles.

RULE
22
Visibility of Lights

WHAT IT MEANS

Type of light*	Vessel length in meters	Visibility in miles
MASTHEAD	under 12	2
	12–20	3
	20–50	5
	over 50	6
SIDE	under 12	1
	12–50	2
	over 50	3
STERN, TOWING, AND ALL-AROUND	under 50	2
	over 50	3

* Note also that inconspicuous, partly submerged vessels or objects being towed should carry a white all-around light, visible at a distance of three miles. *The Inland Rules also specify, for vessels of all lengths, a special flashing light, visible at a distance of two miles.*

Rule 23: Power-Driven Vessels Underway

WHAT IT SAYS

(a) A power-driven vessel underway shall exhibit:

(i) a masthead light forward; *except that a vessel of less than 20 meters in length need not exhibit this light forward of amidships but shall exhibit it as far forward as is practicable;*

(ii) a second masthead light abaft of and higher than the forward one; except that a vessel of less than 50 meters in length shall not be obliged to exhibit such light but may do so;

(iii) sidelights;

(iv) a stern light.

(b) An air-cushion vessel when operating in the nondisplacement mode shall, in addition to the lights prescribed in paragraph (a) of this Rule, exhibit an all-round flashing yellow light *(where it can best be seen).*

(c) A WIG craft only when taking off, landing and in flight near the surface shall, in addition to the lights prescribed in paragraph (a) of this Rule, exhibit a high-intensity all-around flashing red light.

(d) (i) A power-driven vessel of less than 12 meters in length may in lieu of the lights prescribed in paragraph (a) of this Rule exhibit an all-round white light and sidelights;

(ii) a power-driven vessel of less than 7 meters in length whose maximum speed does not exceed 7 knots may in lieu of the lights prescribed in paragraph (a) of this Rule exhibit an all-round white light and shall, if practicable, also exhibit sidelights;

(iii) the masthead light or all-round white light on a power-driven vessel of less than 12 meters in length may be displaced from the fore and aft centerline of the vessel if centerline fitting is not practicable, provided that the sidelights are combined in one lantern which shall be carried on the fore and aft centerline of the vessel or located as nearly as practicable in the same fore and aft line as the masthead light or the all-round white light.

(e) A power-driven vessel when operating on the Great Lakes may carry an all-round white light in lieu of the second masthead light and sternlight prescribed in paragraph (a) of this Rule. The light shall be carried in the position of the second masthead light and be visible at the same minimum range.

WHAT IT MEANS

See illustration on page 34.

Rule 24: Towing and Pushing

WHAT IT SAYS

(a) A power-driven vessel when towing shall exhibit:

(i) instead of the light prescribed in Rule 23(a)(i) or (a)(ii), two masthead lights in a vertical line. When the length of the tow, measuring from the stern of the towing vessel to the after end of the tow exceeds 200 meters, three such lights in a vertical line;

(ii) sidelights;

(iii) a sternlight;

(iv) a towing light in a vertical line above the sternlight;

(v) when the length of the tow exceeds 200 meters, a diamond shape where it can best be seen.

(b) When a pushing vessel and a vessel being pushed ahead are rigidly connected in a composite unit they shall be regarded as a power-driven vessel and exhibit the lights prescribed in Rule 23.

(c) A power-driven vessel when pushing ahead or towing alongside, except in the case of a composite unit *(except as required by paragraphs (b) and (i) of this Rule)*, shall exhibit:

(i) instead of the light prescribed in Rule 23(a)(i) or (a)(ii), two masthead lights in a vertical line;

(ii) sidelights;

(iii) a stern light *(two towing lights in a vertical line)*.

(d) A power-driven vessel to which paragraph (a) or (c) of this Rule apply shall also comply with Rule 23(a)(ii) *(and Rule 23(a)(i))*.

(e) A vessel or object being towed, other than those mentioned in paragraph (g) of this Rule, shall exhibit:

(i) sidelights;

(ii) a sternlight;

(iii) when the length of the tow exceeds 200 meters, a diamond shape where it can best be seen.

(f) Provided that any number of vessels being towed alongside or pushed in a group shall be lighted as one vessel, *except as provided in paragraph (iii).*

(i) a vessel being pushed ahead, not being part of a composite unit, shall exhibit at the forward end, sidelights;

(ii) a vessel being towed alongside shall exhibit a sternlight and at the forward end, sidelights *(and a special flashing light).*

(iii) *when vessels are towed alongside on both sides of the towing vessel a sternlight shall be exhibited on the stern of the outboard vessel on each side of the towing vessel, and a single set of sidelights as far forward and as far outbound as is practicable, and a single, special flashing light.*

RULE

24

Towing and Pushing

(g) An inconspicuous, partly submerged vessel or object, or combination of such vessels or objects being towed, shall exhibit:

(i) if it is less than 25 meters in breadth, one all-round white light at or near the forward end and one at or near the after end except that dracones need not exhibit a light at or near the forward end;

(ii) if it is 25 meters or more in breadth, two additional all-round white lights at or near the extremities of its breadth (*four all-round white lights to mark its length and breadth*);

(iii) if it exceeds 100 meters in length, additional all-round white lights between the lights prescribed in subparagraphs (i) and (ii) so that the distance between the lights shall not exceed 100 meters (*Provided, that any vessels or objects being towed alongside each other shall be lighted as one vessel or object*);

(iv) a diamond shape at or near the aftermost extremity of the last vessel or object being towed and if the length of the tow exceeds 200 meters an additional diamond shape where it can best be seen and located as far forward as is practicable.

(v) the towing vessel may direct a searchlight in the direction of the tow to indicate its presence to an approaching vessel.

(h) Where from any sufficient cause it is impracticable for a vessel or object being towed to exhibit the lights or shapes prescribed in paragraph (e) or (g) of this Rule, all possible measures shall be taken to light the vessel or object towed or at least to indicate the presence of such vessel or object.

(i) Notwithstanding paragraph (c), on the Western Rivers (except below the Huey P. Long Bridge on the Mississippi River) and on waters specified by the Secretary, a power-driven vessel when pushing ahead or towing alongside, except as paragraph (b) applies, shall exhibit:

(i) sidelights; and

(ii) two towing lights in a vertical line.

(i) (*j*) Where from any sufficient cause it is impracticable for a vessel not normally engaged in towing operations to display the lights prescribed in paragraph (a) or (c) of this Rule, such vessel shall not be required to exhibit those lights when engaged in towing another vessel in distress or otherwise in need of assistance. All possible measures shall be taken to indicate the nature of the relationship between the towing vessel and the vessel being towed as authorized by Rule 36, in particular by illuminating the towline.

WHAT IT MEANS

See illustration on page 35.

Rule 25: Sailing Vessels Underway and Vessels Under Oars

WHAT IT SAYS

(a) A sailing vessel underway shall exhibit:

    (i) sidelights;

    (ii) a stern light.

(b) In a sailing vessel of less than 20 meters in length the lights prescribed in paragraph (a) of this Rule may be combined in one lantern carried at or near the top of the mast where it can best be seen.

(c) A sailing vessel underway may, in addition to the lights prescribed in paragraph (a) of this Rule, exhibit at or near the top of the mast, where they can best be seen, two all-round lights in a vertical line, the upper being red and the lower green, but these lights shall not be exhibited in conjunction with the combined lantern permitted by paragraph (b) of this Rule.

(d) (i) A sailing vessel of less than 7 meters in length shall, if practicable, exhibit the lights prescribed in paragraph (a) or (b) of this Rule, but if she does not, she shall have ready at hand an electric torch or lighted lantern showing a white light which shall be exhibited in sufficient time to prevent collision.

    (ii) A vessel under oars may exhibit the lights prescribed in this Rule for sailing vessels, but if she does not, she shall have ready at hand an electric torch or lighted lantern showing a white light which shall be exhibited in sufficient time to prevent collision.

(e) A vessel proceeding under sail when also being propelled by machinery shall exhibit forward where it can best be seen a conical shape, apex downwards. *(A vessel of less than 12 meters in length is not required to exhibit this shape, but may do so.)*

RULE 25
Sailing Vessels Underway and Vessels Under Oars

WHAT IT MEANS

See illustration on page 36.

Rule 26: Fishing Vessels

RULE
26
Fishing Vessels

WHAT IT SAYS

(a) A vessel engaged in fishing, whether underway or at anchor, shall exhibit only the lights and shapes prescribed in this Rule.

(b) A vessel when engaged in trawling, by which is meant the dragging through the water of a dredge net or other apparatus used as a fishing appliance, shall exhibit:

(i) two all-round lights in a vertical line, the upper being green and the lower white, or a shape consisting of two cones with their apexes together in a vertical line one above the other;

(ii) a masthead light abaft of and higher than the all-round green light; a vessel of less than 50 meters in length shall not be obliged to exhibit such a light but may do so;

(iii) when making way through the water, in addition to the lights prescribed in this paragraph, sidelights and a sternlight.

(c) A vessel engaged in fishing, other than trawling, shall exhibit:

(i) two all-round lights in a vertical line, the upper being red and the lower white, or a shape consisting of two cones with apexes together in a vertical line one above the other;

(ii) when there is outlying gear extending more than 150 meters horizontally from the vessel, an all-round white light or a cone apex upward in the direction of the gear; and

(iii) when making way through the water, in addition to the lights prescribed in this paragraph, sidelights and a sternlight.

(d) The additional signals described in Annex II to these regulations apply to a vessel engaged in fishing in close proximity to other vessels engaged in fishing.

(e) A vessel when not engaged in fishing shall not exhibit the lights or shapes prescribed in this Rule, but only those prescribed for a vessel of her length.

WHAT IT MEANS

See illustration on page 37.

Rule 27: Vessels Not Under Command or Restricted in Their Ability to Maneuver

WHAT IT SAYS

(a) A vessel not under command shall exhibit:

    (i) two all-round red lights in a vertical line where they can best be seen;

    (ii) two balls or similar shapes in a vertical line where they can best be seen;

    (iii) when making way through the water, in addition to the lights prescribed in this paragraph, sidelights and a sternlight.

(b) A vessel restricted in her ability to maneuver, except a vessel engaged in mine-clearance operations, shall exhibit:

    (i) three all-round lights in a vertical line where they can best be seen. The highest and lowest of these lights shall be red and the middle light shall be white;

    (ii) three shapes in a vertical line where they can best be seen. The highest and lowest of these shapes shall be balls and the middle one a diamond;

    (iii) when making way through the water, a masthead light or lights, sidelights and a sternlight, in addition to the lights prescribed in subparagraph (b) (i);

    (iv) when at anchor, in addition to the lights or shapes prescribed in subparagraphs (b) (i) and (ii), the light, lights or shape prescribed in Rule 30.

(c) A power-driven vessel engaged in a towing operation such as severely restricts the towing vessel and her tow in their ability to deviate from their course shall, in addition to the lights or shapes prescribed in Rule 24(a), exhibit the lights or shapes prescribed in sub-paragraphs (b)(i) and (ii) of this Rule,

(d) A vessel engaged in dredging or underwater operations, when restricted in her ability to maneuver, shall exhibit the lights and shapes prescribed in subparagraphs (b)(i), (ii) and (iii) of this Rule and shall in addition, when an obstruction exists, exhibit:

    (i) two all-round red lights or two balls in a vertical line to indicate the side on which the obstruction exists;

    (ii) two all-round green lights or two diamonds in a vertical line to indicate the side on which another vessel may pass;

    (iii) when at anchor, the lights or shapes prescribed in this paragraph instead of the lights or shape prescribed in Rule 30 *(for anchored vessels).*

(e) Whenever the size of a vessel engaged in diving operations makes it impracticable to exhibit all lights and shapes prescribed in paragraph (d) of this Rule, the following shall be exhibited:

    (i) three all-round lights in a vertical line where they can best be seen. The highest and lowest of these lights shall be red and the middle light shall be white;

RULE

27

Vessels Not Under Command or Restricted in Their Ability to Maneuver

RULE 27

Vessels Not Under Command or Restricted in Their Ability to Maneuver

(ii) a rigid replica of the International Code flag "A" not less than 1 meter in height. Measures shall be taken to ensure its all round visibility.

(f) A vessel engaged in mine-clearance operations shall in addition to the lights prescribed for a power-driven vessel in Rule 23 or to the lights or shape prescribed for a vessel at anchor in Rule 30 as appropriate, exhibit three all-round green lights or three balls. One of these lights or shapes shall be exhibited near the foremast head and one at each end of the fore yard. These lights or shapes indicate that it is dangerous for another vessel to approach within 1000 meters of the mine-clearance vessel.

(g) Vessels of less than 12 meters in length, except those engaged in diving operations, shall not be required to exhibit the lights and shapes prescribed in this Rule.

(h) The signals prescribed in this Rule are not signals of vessels in distress and requiring assistance. Such signals are contained in Annex IV to these Regulations.

WHAT IT MEANS

See illustration on page 38.

Rule 28: Vessels Constrained by Their Draft

WHAT IT SAYS

RULE 28

Vessels Constrained by Their Draft

A vessel constrained by her draft may, in addition to the lights prescribed for power-driven vessels in Rule 23, exhibit where they can best be seen three all-round red lights in a vertical line, or a cylinder. *Note: There is no mention of a "vessel constrained by her draft" in the Inland Rules.*

WHAT IT MEANS

See illustration on page 39.

Rule 29: Pilot Vessels

WHAT IT SAYS

(a) A vessel engaged on pilotage duty shall exhibit:

> (i) at or near the masthead, two all-round lights in a vertical line, the upper being white and the lower red;
>
> (ii) when underway, in addition, sidelights and a sternlight;
>
> (iii) when at anchor, in addition to the lights prescribed in subparagraph (i), the light, lights or shape prescribed in Rule 30 for vessels at anchor.

(b) A pilot vessel when not engaged on pilotage duty shall exhibit the lights or shapes prescribed for a similar vessel of her length.

RULE
29
Pilot Vessels

WHAT IT MEANS

See illustration on page 39.

Rule 30: Anchored Vessels and Vessels Aground

WHAT IT SAYS

(a) A vessel at anchor shall exhibit where it can best be seen:

> (i) in the fore part, an all-round white light or one ball;
>
> (ii) at or near the stern and at a lower level than the light prescribed in subparagraph (i), an all-round white light.

(b) A vessel of less than 50 meters in length may exhibit an all-round white light where it can best be seen instead of the lights prescribed in paragraph (a) of this Rule.

(c) A vessel at anchor may, and a vessel of 100 meters and more in length shall, also use the available working or equivalent lights to illuminate her decks.

(d) A vessel aground shall exhibit the lights prescribed in paragraph (a) or (b) of this Rule and in addition, *(if practicable)* where they can best be seen:

> (i) two all-round red lights in a vertical line;
>
> (ii) three balls in a vertical line.

(e) A vessel of less than 7 meters in length, when at anchor, not in or near a narrow channel, fairway or anchorage, or where other vessels normally navigate, shall not be required to exhibit the lights or shape prescribed in paragraphs (a) and (b) of this Rule.

RULE
30
Anchored Vessels and Vessels Aground

RULE
30

Anchored Vessels and Vessels Aground

(f) A vessel of less than 12 meters in length, when aground, shall not be required to exhibit the lights or shapes prescribed in subparagraphs (d)(i) and (ii) of this Rule.

(g) A vessel of less than 20 meters in length, when at anchor in a special anchorage area designated by the Secretary, shall not be required to exhibit the anchor lights and shapes required by this Rule.

WHAT IT MEANS

See illustration on page 40.

Rule 31: Seaplanes

WHAT IT SAYS

RULE
31

Seaplanes

Where it is impracticable for a seaplane, or a WIG craft to exhibit lights and shapes of the characteristics or in the positions prescribed in the Rules of this Part she shall exhibit lights and shapes as closely similar in characteristics and position as is possible.

WHAT IT MEANS

See illustration on page 40.

Sound and Light Signals

Rule 32: Definitions

WHAT IT SAYS

RULE
32

Definitions

(a) The word "whistle" means any sound signaling appliance capable of producing the prescribed blasts and which complies with the specifications in Annex III to these Regulations.

(b) The term "short blast" means a blast of about one second's duration.

(c) The term "prolonged blast" means a blast of from four to six seconds' duration.

WHAT IT MEANS

Short blast: one second (·)

Prolonged blast: four to six seconds (—)

Whistle: sound device meeting the following specifications.

Length	Hertz	Decibels	Range
12 m to 20 m	280–700 *(250–525)*	120	0.5 nm
20 m to 75 m	280–700 *(250–525)*	130	1.0 nm

RULE 32

Definitions

Rule 33: Equipment for Sound Signals

WHAT IT SAYS

(a) A vessel of 12 meters or more in length shall be provided with a whistle, a vessel of 20 meters or more in length shall be provided with a bell in addition to a whistle, and a vessel of 100 meters or more in length shall, in addition, be provided with a gong, the tone and sound of which cannot be confused with that of the bell. The whistle, bell and gong shall comply with the specifications in Annex III to these Regulations. The bell or gong or both may be replaced by other equipment having the same respective sound characteristics, provided that manual sounding of the prescribed signals shall always be possible.

(b) A vessel of less than 12 meters in length shall not be obliged to carry the sound-signaling appliances prescribed in paragraph (a) of this Rule but if she does not, she shall be provided with some other means of making an efficient sound signal.

RULE 33

Equipment for Sound Signals

WHAT IT MEANS

The type of required sound-making apparatus depends on the length of the vessel.

Length	Any	Whistle	Bell	Gong
<12 m	✔			
12 m to <20 m		✔		
20 m to <100 m		✔	✔	
≥100 m		✔	✔	✔

Rule 34: Maneuvering and Warning Signals

WHAT IT SAYS

RULE
34
Maneuvering
and Warning
Signals

(a) When vessels are in sight of one another, a power-driven vessel underway, when maneuvering as authorized or required by these Rules, shall indicate that maneuver by the following signals on her whistle:

—one short blast to mean "I am altering my course to starboard";

—two short blasts to mean "I am altering my course to port";

—three short blasts to mean "I am operating astern propulsion."

(b) Any vessel may supplement the whistle signals prescribed in paragraph (a) of this Rule by light signals, repeated as appropriate, while the maneuver is being carried out:

(i) these light signals shall have the following significance:

— one flash to mean "I am altering my course to starboard";

— two flashes to mean "I am altering my course to port";

— three flashes to mean "I am operating astern propulsion";

(ii) the duration of each flash shall be about one second, the interval between flashes shall be about one second, and the interval between successive signals shall be not less than ten seconds;

(iii) the light used for this signal shall, if fitted, be an all-round white light, visible at a minimum range of 5 miles *(2 miles synchronized with a whistle),* and shall comply with the provisions of Annex I to these Regulations.

The italicized text indicates where the Inland Rules differ substantially from the COLREGS.

(c) When in sight of one another in a narrow channel or fairway:

(i) a vessel intending to overtake another shall in compliance with Rule 9(e)(i) indicate her intention by the following signals on her whistle:

— two prolonged blasts followed by one short blast to mean "I intend to overtake you on your starboard side";

— two prolonged blasts followed by two short blasts to mean "I intend to overtake you on your port side."

(ii) the vessel about to be overtaken when acting in accordance with Rule 9(e)(i) shall indicate her agreement by the following signal on her whistle:

— one prolonged, one short, one prolonged and one short blast, in that order.

(d) When vessels in sight of one another are approaching each other and from any cause either vessel fails to understand the intentions or actions of the other, or is in doubt whether sufficient action is being taken by the other to avoid collision, the vessel in doubt shall immediately indicate such doubt by giving at least five short and rapid blasts on the whistle. Such signal may be supplemented by a light signal of at least five short and rapid flashes.

(e) A vessel nearing a bend or an area of a channel or fairway where other vessels may be obscured by an intervening obstruction shall sound one prolonged blast. Such signal shall be answered with a prolonged blast by any approaching vessel that may be within hearing around the bend or behind the intervening obstruction.

(f) If whistles are fitted on a vessel at a distance apart of more than 100 meters, one whistle only shall be used for giving maneuvering and warning signals.

RULE
34
Maneuvering and Warning Signals

(a) *When power-driven vessels are in sight of one another and meeting or crossing at a distance within half a mile of each other, each vessel underway, when maneuvering as authorized or required by these Rules:*

> *(i) shall indicate that maneuver by the following signals on her whistle: one short blast to mean "I intend to leave you on my port side"; two short blasts to mean "I intend to leave you on my starboard side"; and three short blasts to mean "I am operating astern propulsion."*

> *(ii) upon hearing the one or two blast signal of the other shall, if in agreement, sound the same whistle signal and take the steps necessary to effect a safe passing. If, however, from any cause, the vessel doubts the safety of the proposed maneuver, she shall sound the danger signal specified in paragraph (d) of this Rule and each vessel shall take appropriate precautionary action until a safe passing agreement is made.*

(b) *A vessel may supplement the whistle signals prescribed in paragraph (a) of this Rule by light signals:*

> *(i) These signals shall have the following significance: one flash to mean "I intend to leave you on my port side"; two flashes to mean "I intend to leave you on my starboard side"; three flashes to mean "I am operating astern propulsion";*

> *(ii) The duration of each flash shall be about 1 second; and*

> *(iii) The light used for this signal shall, if fitted, be one all-round white or yellow light, visible at a minimum range of 2 miles, synchronized with the whistle, and shall comply with the provisions of Annex I to these Rules.*

(c) *When in sight of one another:*

> *(i) a power-driven vessel intending to overtake another power-driven vessel shall indicate her intention by the following signals on her whistle: one short blast to mean "I intend to overtake you on your starboard side"; two short blasts to mean "I intend to overtake you on your port side"; and*

> *(ii) the power-driven vessel about to be overtaken shall, if in agreement, sound a similar sound signal. If in doubt she shall sound the danger signal prescribed in paragraph (d).*

(d) *When vessels in sight of one another are approaching each other and from any cause either vessel fails to understand the intentions or actions of the other, or is in doubt whether sufficient action is being taken by the other to avoid collision, the vessel in doubt shall immediately indicate such doubt by giving at least five short and rapid blasts on the whistle. This signal may be supplemented by a light signal of at least five short and rapid flashes.*

(e) *A vessel nearing a bend or an area of a channel or fairway where other vessels may be obscured*

**RULE
34
Maneuvering
and Warning
Signals**

by an intervening obstruction shall sound one prolonged blast. This signal shall be answered with a prolonged blast by any approaching vessel that may be within hearing around the bend or behind the intervening obstruction.

(f) If whistles are fitted on a vessel at a distance apart of more than 100 meters, one whistle only shall be used for giving maneuvering and warning signals.

(g) When a power-driven vessel is leaving a dock or berth, she shall sound one prolonged blast.

(h) A vessel that reaches agreement with another vessel in a meeting, crossing, or overtaking situation by using the radiotelephone as prescribed by the Bridge-to-Bridge Radiotelephone Act (85 Stat. 165; 33 U.S.C. 1207), is not obliged to sound the whistle signals prescribed by this Rule, but may do so. If agreement is not reached, then whistle signals shall be exchanged in a timely manner and shall prevail.

WHAT IT MEANS

Maneuvering and Warning Signals in Sight   (• = one-second blast; — = four- to six-second blast)

INTERNATIONAL (ACTION BEING TAKEN) MEETING OR CROSSING AND ACTION IS REQUIRED (NO ANSWER REQUIRED):		INLAND (ACTION PROPOSED TO BE TAKEN) MEETING OR CROSSING WITHIN ½ MILE OF EACH OTHER AND ACTION IS REQUIRED (AGREEMENT BY SAME SIGNAL REQUIRED):	
I am altering course to starboard	•	I propose leaving you to port	•
I am altering course to port	• •	I propose leaving you to starboard	• •
I am operating astern propulsion	• • •	I am operating astern propulsion	• • •
OVERTAKING IN A NARROW CHANNEL OR FAIRWAY AND ACTION IS REQUIRED (AGREEMENT REQUIRED BEFORE ACTION):		OVERTAKING IN A NARROW CHANNEL OR FAIRWAY AND ACTION IS REQUIRED (AGREEMENT BY SAME SIGNAL REQUIRED BEFORE ACTION):	
I intend to overtake on your starboard	— — •	I propose overtaking on your starboard	•
I intend to overtake on your port	— — • •	I propose overtaking on your port	• •
I agree to be overtaken	— • — •	I agree to be overtaken	• or • •
Warning—I don't understand your intentions	• • • • •	Warning—I don't understand your intentions	• • • • •
Approaching a bend in a channel	—	Approaching a bend in a channel or leaving berth or dock	—

Rule 35: Sound Signals in Restricted Visibility

WHAT IT SAYS

In or near an area of restricted visibility, whether by day or night, the signals prescribed in this Rule shall be used as follows:

(a) A power-driven vessel making way through the water shall sound at intervals of not more than 2 minutes one prolonged blast.

(b) A power-driven vessel underway but stopped and making no way through the water shall sound at intervals of not more than 2 minutes two prolonged blasts in succession with an interval of about 2 seconds between them.

(c) A vessel not under command, a vessel restricted in her ability to maneuver, a vessel constrained by her draft, a sailing vessel, a vessel engaged in fishing *(whether underway or at anchor)* and a vessel engaged in towing or pushing another vessel shall, instead of the signals prescribed in paragraphs (a) or (b) of this Rule, sound at intervals of not more than 2 minutes three blasts in succession, namely one prolonged followed by two short blasts.

(d) A vessel engaged in fishing, when at anchor, and a vessel restricted in her ability to maneuver when carrying out her work at anchor, shall instead of the signals prescribed in paragraph (g) of this Rule sound the signal prescribed in paragraph (c) of this Rule. *(Note that this paragraph does not exist in the Inland Rules.)*

(e) *(d)* A vessel towed or if more than one vessel is towed the last vessel of the tow, if manned, shall at intervals of not more than 2 minutes sound four blasts in succession, namely one prolonged followed by three short blasts. When practicable, this signal shall be made immediately after the signal made by the towing vessel.

(f) *(e)* When a pushing vessel and a vessel being pushed ahead are rigidly connected in a composite unit they shall be regarded as a power-driven vessel and shall give the signals prescribed in paragraphs (a) or (b) of this Rule.

(g) *(f)* A vessel at anchor shall at intervals of not more than one minute ring the bell rapidly for about 5 seconds. In a vessel of 100 meters or more in length the bell shall be sounded in the forepart of the vessel and immediately after the ringing of the bell the gong shall be sounded rapidly for about 5 seconds in the after part of the vessel. A vessel at anchor may in addition sound three blasts in succession, namely one short, one prolonged and one short blast, to give warning of her position and of the possibility of collision to an approaching vessel.

(h) *(g)* A vessel aground shall give the bell signal and if required the gong signal prescribed in paragraph (g) *(f)* of this Rule and shall, in addition, give three separate and distinct strokes on the bell immediately before and after the rapid ringing of the bell. A vessel aground may in addition sound an appropriate whistle signal.

(i) *(h)* A vessel of 12 meters or more but less than 20 meters in length shall not be obliged to

RULE

35

Sound Signals in Restricted Visibility

give the bell signals prescribed in paragraphs (g) and (h) of this Rule. However, if she does not, she shall make some other efficient sound signal at interval of not more than 2 minutes.

(j) A vessel of less than 12 meters in length shall not be obliged to give the above-mentioned signals but, if she does not, shall make some other efficient sound signal at intervals of not more than 2 minutes.

(k)(i) A pilot vessel when engaged on pilotage duty may in addition to the signals prescribed in paragraphs (a), (b) or (g) (f) of this Rule sound an identity signal consisting of four short blasts.

(j) The following vessels shall not be required to sound signals as prescribed in paragraph (f) of this Rule when anchored in a special anchorage area designated by the Secretary:

(i) a vessel of less than 20 meters in length; and

(ii) a barge, canal boat, scow, or other nondescript craft.

WHAT IT MEANS

Sound Signals in Restricted Visibility

(• = one-second blast; — = four- to six-second blast. Repeat every two minutes, maximum.)

Power vessel making way	—
Power vessel stopped	— —
Manned tow	— • • •
Pilot vessel—optional	• • • •
Not under command, restricted in ability to maneuver, constrained by draft, sailing, fishing, towing or pushing, fishing at anchor, restricted at anchor	— • •

ANCHORED:

Less than 100 meters—ring bell rapidly for five seconds every minute

Greater than or equal to 100 meters—ring bell five seconds fore, then gong five seconds aft

Additional option   • — •

AGROUND:

Three distinct claps of bell + rapid five-second bell + three claps, all repeated at one minute

Vessel less than twenty meters anchored or aground option: any sound at two minutes

Rule 36: Signals to Attract Attention

WHAT IT SAYS

If necessary to attract the attention of another vessel, any vessel may make light or sound signals that cannot be mistaken for any signal authorized elsewhere in these Rules, or may direct the beam of her searchlight in the direction of the danger, in such a way as not to embarrass any vessel. Any light to attract the attention of another vessel shall be such that it cannot be mistaken for any aid to navigation. For the purpose of this rule the use of high intensity intermittent or revolving lights, such as strobe lights, shall be avoided. *(The prohibition of strobes does not apply to Inland Rules.)*

RULE 36 Signals to Attract Attention

WHAT IT MEANS

In attracting the attention of another vessel, you may use any light or sound signal that cannot be mistaken for any of the signals given in the Rules. The only exception is a prohibition of high intensity flashing or revolving lights, such as strobes, in the International Rules. *The prohibition of strobes does not apply to Inland Rules.*

Rule 37: Distress Signals

WHAT IT SAYS

When a vessel is in distress and requires assistance she shall use or exhibit the signals in Annex IV to these Regulations. *The distress signals for Inland waters are the same as those for International waters with the following additional signal described: A high-intensity white light flashing at regular intervals from 50 to 70 times per minute. See page 41.*

RULE 37 Distress Signals

WHAT IT MEANS

Vessels in distress and requiring assistance shall use one or more of the distress signals listed in Annex IV of the Rules (see page 112). *The only exception is permission to use strobes in Inland waters. (See page 41.)*

Rule 38: Exemptions

RULE
38
Exemptions

Any vessel (or class of vessels) provided that she complies with the requirements of the International Regulations for Preventing Collisions at Sea, 1960, the keel of which is laid or which is at a corresponding stage of construction before the entry into force of these Regulations may be exempted from compliance therewith as follows:

(a) The installation of lights with ranges prescribed in Rule 22, until four years after the date of entry into force of these Regulations, except that vessels of less than 20 m in length are permanently exempt.

(b) The installation of lights with color specifications as prescribed in Section 7 of Annex I to these Regulations, until four years after the date of entry into force of these Regulations.

(c) The repositioning of lights as a result of conversion from Imperial to metric units and rounding off measurement figures, permanent exemption.

(d) (i) The repositioning of masthead lights on vessels of less than 150 m in length, resulting from the prescriptions of Section 3(a) of Annex I to these Regulations, permanent exemption.

(ii) The repositioning of masthead lights on vessels of 150 m or more in length, resulting from the prescriptions of Section 3(a) of Annex I to these Regulations, until 9 years after the date of entry into force of these Regulations.

(e) The repositioning of masthead lights resulting from the prescriptions of Section 2(b) of Annex I to these Regulations, until 9 years after the date of entry into force of these Regulations.

(f) The repositioning of sidelights resulting from the prescriptions of Sections 2(g) and 3(b) of Annex I to these Regulations, until 9 years after the date of entry into force of these Regulations.

(g) The requirements for sound signal appliances prescribed in Annex III to these Regulations, until 9 years after the date of entry into force of these Regulations.

(h) The repositioning of all-round lights resulting from the prescription of Section 9(b) of Annex I to these Regulations, permanent exemption.

— INLAND —

Any vessel or class of vessels, the keel of which is laid or which is at a corresponding stage of construction before the date of enactment of this Act, provided that she complies with the requirements of—

(a) The Act of June 7, 1897 (30 Stat. 96), as amended (33 U.S.C. 154-232) for vessels navigating the waters subject to that statute;

(b) Section 4233 of the Revised Statutes (33 U.S.C. 301-356) for vessels navigating the waters subject to that statute;

(c) The Act of February 8, 1895 (28 Stat. 645), as amended (33 U.S.C. 241-295) for vessels navigating the waters subject to that statute; or

(d) Sections 3, 4, and 5 of the Act of April 25, 1940 (54 Stat. 163), as amended (46 U.S.C. 526 b, c, and d) for motorboats navigating the waters subject to that statute; shall be exempted from compliance with the technical Annexes to these Rules as follows:

(i) the installation of lights with ranges prescribed in Rule 22, until 4 years after the effective date of these Rules, except that vessels of less than 20 m in length are permanently exempt;

(ii) the installation of lights with color specifications as prescribed in Annex I to these Rules, until 4 years after the effective date of these Rules, except that vessels of less than 20 m in length are permanently exempt;

(iii) the repositioning of lights as a result of conversion to metric units and rounding off measurement figures, are permanently exempt; and.

(iv) the horizontal repositioning of masthead lights prescribed by Annex I to these Rules:

(1) on vessels of less than 150 m in length, permanent exemption.

(2) on vessels of 150 m or more in length, until 9 years after the effective date of these Rules.

(v) the restructuring or repositioning of all lights to meet the prescriptions of Annex I to these Rules, until 9 years after the effective date of these Rules;

(vi) power-driven vessels of 12 m or more but less than 20 m in length are permanently exempt from the provisions of Rule 23(a)(i) and 23 (a)(iv) provided that, in place of these lights, the vessel exhibits a white light aft visible all round the horizon; and

(vii) the requirements for sound signal appliances prescribed in Annex III to these Rules, until 9 years after the effective date of these Rules.

Annex I: Positioning and Technical Details of Lights and Shapes

1. Definition

(a) The term "height above the hull" means height above the uppermost continuous deck. This height shall be measured from the position vertically beneath the location of the light.

(b) High-speed craft means a craft capable of maximum speed in meters per second (m/s) equal to or exceeding: $3.7\nabla^{0.1667}$; where ∇ = displacement corresponding to the design waterline (meters^3).

(c) The term "practical cut-off" means, for vessels 20 m or more in length, 12.5 percent of the minimum luminous intensity (Table 84.15(b)) corresponding to the greatest range of visibility for which the requirements of Annex I are met.

(d) The term "Rule" or "Rules" means the Inland Navigation Rules contained in Sec. 2 of the Inland Navigational Rules Act of 1980 (Pub. L. 96-591, 94 Stat. 3415, 33 U.S.C. 2001, December 24, 1980) as amended.

2. Vertical positioning and spacing of lights

(a) On a power-driven vessel of 20 m or more the masthead lights shall be placed as follows:

(i) the forward masthead light, or if only one masthead light is carried, then that light, at a height above the hull of not less than 6 m, and, if the breadth of the vessel exceeds 6 m, then at a height above the hull not less than such breadth, so however that the light need not be placed at a greater height above the hull than 12 m;

The forward masthead light, or if only one masthead light is carried, then that light, at a height above the hull of not less than 5 m, and, if the breadth of the vessel exceeds 5 m, then at a height above the hull not less than such breadth, so however that the light need not be placed at a greater height above the hull than 8 m;

(ii) when two masthead lights are carried the after one shall be at least 4.5 m vertically higher than the forward one.

When two masthead lights are carried the after one shall be at least 2 m vertically higher than the forward one.

(b) The vertical separation of masthead lights of power-driven vessels shall be such that in all normal conditions of trim the after light will be seen over and separate from the forward light at a distance of 1000 m from the stem when viewed from sea level.

(c) The masthead light of a power-driven vessel of 12 m but less than 20 m in length shall be placed at a height above the gunwale of not less than 2.5 m.

(d) A power-driven vessel of less than 12 m in length may carry the uppermost light at a height of less than 2.5 m above the gunwale. When however a masthead light is carried in addition to sidelights and a sternlight, then such masthead light shall be carried at least 1 m higher than the sidelights.

The masthead light, or the all-round light described in Rule 23(c), of a power-driven vessel of less than 12 m in length shall be carried at least 1 m higher than the sidelights.

(e) One of the two or three masthead lights prescribed for a power-driven vessel when engaged in towing or pushing another vessel shall be placed in the same position as either the forward masthead light or the after masthead light; provided that, if carried on the aftermast, the lowest after masthead light shall be at least 4.5 m vertically higher than the forward masthead light.

One of the two or three masthead lights prescribed for a power-driven vessel when engaged in towing or pushing another vessel shall be placed in the same position as either the forward masthead light or the after masthead light, provided that the lowest after masthead light shall be at least 2 m vertically higher than the highest forward masthead light.

(f)(i) The masthead light or lights prescribed in Rule 23(a) shall be so placed as to be above and clear of all other lights and obstructions except as described in subparagraph (ii).

> (ii) When it is impracticable to carry the all-round lights prescribed by Rule 27(b)(i) or Rule 28 below the masthead lights, they may be carried above the after masthead light(s) or vertically in between the forward masthead light(s) and after masthead light(s), provided that in the latter case the requirement of Section 3(c) *§84.05(d)* of this Annex shall be complied with.

(g) The sidelights of a power-driven vessel shall be placed at a height above the hull not greater than three quarters of that of the forward masthead light. They shall not be so low as to be interfered with by deck lights.

The sidelights of a power-driven vessel shall be placed at least 1 m lower than the forward masthead light. They shall not be so low as to be interfered with by deck lights.

(h) The sidelights, if in a combined lantern and carried on a power-driven vessel of less than 20 m in length, shall be placed not less than 1 m below the masthead light.

[Reserved in Inland Rules]

(i) When the Rules prescribe two or three lights to be carried in a vertical line, they shall be spaced as follows:

> (i) on a vessel of 20 m in length or more such lights shall be spaced not less than 2 m apart, and the lowest of these lights shall, except where a towing light is required, be placed at a height of not less than 4 m above the hull;
>
> *On a vessel of 20 m in length or more such lights shall be spaced not less than 1 m apart, and the lowest of these lights shall, except where a towing light is required, be placed at a height of not less than 4 m above the hull;*
>
> (ii) on a vessel of less than 20 m in length such lights shall be spaced not less than 1 m apart and the lowest of these lights shall, except where a towing light is required, be placed at a height of not less than 2 m above the hull *(gunwales)*;
>
> (iii) when three lights are carried they shall be equally spaced.

(j) The lower of the two all-round lights prescribed for a vessel when engaged in fishing shall be at a height above the sidelights not less than twice the distance between the two vertical lights.

(k) The forward anchor light prescribed in Rule 30(a)(i), when two are carried, shall not be less than 4.5 m above the after one. On a vessel of 50 m or more in length this forward anchor light shall be placed at a height of not less than 6 m above the hull.

3. Horizontal positioning and spacing of lights

(a) When two masthead lights are prescribed for a power-driven vessel, the horizontal distance between them shall not be less than one half of the length of the vessel but need not be more than 100 m. The forward light shall be placed not more than one quarter of the length of the vessel from the stem.

Except as specified in paragraph (e) of this section, when two masthead lights are prescribed for a power-driven vessel, the horizontal distance between them shall not be less than one quarter of the length of the vessel but need not be more than 50 m. The forward light shall be placed not more than one half of the length of the vessel from the stem.

(b) On a power-driven vessel of 20 m or more in length the sidelights shall not be placed in front of the forward masthead lights. They shall be placed at or near the side of the vessel.

(c) When the lights prescribed in Rule 27(b)(i) or Rule 28 are placed vertically between the forward masthead light(s) and the after masthead light(s) these all-round lights shall be placed at a horizontal distance of not less than 2 m from the fore and aft centerline of the vessel in the athwart ship direction.

(d) (Inland only) When only one masthead light is prescribed for a power-driven vessel, this light shall be exhibited forward of amidships; except that a vessel of less than 20 meters in length need not exhibit this light forward of amidships but shall exhibit it as far forward as is practicable.

(e) (Inland only) On power-driven vessels 50 m but less than 60 m in length operated on the Western Rivers, and those waters specified in §89.25, the horizontal distance between masthead lights shall not be less than 10 m.

4. Details of location of direction-indicating lights for fishing vessels, dredgers and vessels engaged in underwater operations

(a) The light indicating the direction of the outlying gear from a vessel engaged in fishing as prescribed in Rule 26(c)(ii) shall be placed at a horizontal distance of not less than 2 m and not more than 6 m away from the two all-round red and white lights. This light shall be placed not higher than the all-round white light prescribed in Rule 26(c)(i) and not lower than the sidelights.

(b) The lights and shapes on a vessel engaged in dredging or underwater operations to indicate the obstructed side and/or the side on which it is safe to pass, as prescribed in Rule 27(d)(i) and (ii), shall be placed at the maximum practical horizontal distance, but in no case less than 2 m, from the lights or shapes prescribed in Rule 27(b)(i) and (ii). In no case shall the upper of these lights or shapes be at a greater height than the lower of the three lights or shapes prescribed in Rule 27(b)(i) and (ii).

5. Screens for sidelights

The sidelights of vessels of 20 m or more in length shall be fitted with inboard screens painted matt black, and meeting the requirements of Section 9 *§84.17* of this Annex. On vessels of less than 20 m in length the sidelights, if necessary to meet the requirements of Section 9 *§84.17* of this Annex, shall be fitted with inboard matt black screens. With a combined lantern, using a single vertical filament and a very narrow division between the green and red sections, external screens need not be fitted.

(Inland only) On power-driven vessels less than 12 m in length constructed after July 31, 1983, the masthead light, or the all-round light described in Rule 23(c) shall be screened to prevent direct illumination of the vessel forward of the operator's position.

6. Shapes

(a) Shapes shall be black and of the following sizes:

    (i) a ball shall have a diameter of not less than 0.6 m;

    (ii) a cone shall have a base diameter of not less than 0.6 m and a height equal to its diameter;

    (iii) a cylinder shall have a diameter of at least 0.6 m and a height of twice its diameter; *(no cylinder in Inland Rules).*

    (iv) a diamond shape shall consist of two cones as defined in (ii) *(a)(2)* above having a common base.

(b) The vertical distance between shapes shall be at least 1.5 m.

(c) In a vessel of less than 20 m in length shapes of lesser dimensions but commensurate with the size of the vessel may be used and the distance apart may be correspondingly reduced.

7. Color specification of lights

The chromaticity of all navigation lights shall conform to the following standards, which lie within the boundaries of the area of the diagram specified for each color by the International Commission on Illumination (CIE).

The boundaries of the area for each color are given by indicating the corner coordinates, which are as follows:

(i) White:

x	0.525	0.525	0.452	0.310	0.310	0.443
y	0.382	0.440	0.440	0.348	0.283	0.382

(ii) Green:

x	0.028	0.009	0.300	0.203
y	0.385	0.723	0.511	0.356

(iii) Red:

x	0.680	0.660	0.735	0.721
y	0.320	0.320	0.265	0.259

(iv) Yellow:

x	0.612	0.618	0.575	0.575
y	0.382	0.382	0.425	0.406

8. Intensity of lights

(a) The minimum luminous intensity of lights shall be calculated by using the formula:

$$I = 3.43 \times 10^6 \times T \times D^2 \times K^{-D}$$

where   I is luminous intensity in candelas under service conditions

T is threshold factor 2×10^{-7} lux,

D is range of visibility (luminous range) of the light in nautical miles,

K is atmospheric transmissivity. For prescribed lights the value of K shall be 0.8, corresponding to a meteorological visibility of approximately 13 nautical miles.

(b) A selection of figures derived from the formula is given in the following table:

Range of visibility (luminous range) of light in nm, D	Luminous intensity of light in candelas for K = 0.8, I
1	0.9
2	4.3
3	12
4	27
5	52
6	94

Note: The maximum luminous intensity of navigation lights should be limited to avoid undue glare. This shall not be achieved by a variable control of the luminous intensity.

9. Horizontal sectors

(a)(i) In the forward direction, sidelights as fitted on the vessel shall show the minimum required intensities. The intensities shall decrease to reach practical cut-off between 1 degree and 3 degrees outside the prescribed sectors.

(ii) For sternlights and masthead lights and at 22.5 degrees abaft the beam for sidelights, the minimum required intensities shall be maintained over the arc of the horizon up to 5 degrees within the limits of the sectors prescribed in Rule 21. From 5 degrees within the prescribed sectors the intensity may decrease by 50 percent up to the prescribed limits; it shall decrease steadily to reach practical cut-off at not more than 5 degrees outside the prescribed sectors.

(b)(i) All-round lights shall be so located as not to be obscured by masts, topmasts or structures within angular sectors of more than 6 degrees, except anchor lights prescribed in Rule 30, which need not be placed at an impracticable height above the hull, *and the all-round white light described in Rule 23(d), which may not be obscured at all.*

(ii) If it is impracticable to comply with paragraph (b)(i) of this section by exhibiting only one all-round light, two all-round lights shall be used suitably positioned or screened so that they appear, as far as practicable, as one light at a distance of one mile.

10. Vertical sectors

(a) The vertical sectors of electric lights as fitted, with the exception of lights on sailing vessels underway, *and on unmanned barges,* shall ensure that:

(i) at least the required minimum intensity is maintained at all angles from 5 degrees above to 5 degrees below the horizontal;

(ii) at least 60 percent of the required minimum intensity is maintained from 7.5 degrees above to 7.5 degrees below the horizontal.

(b) In the case of sailing vessels underway the vertical sectors of electric lights as fitted shall ensure that:

(i) at least the required minimum intensity is maintained at all angles from 5 degrees above to 5 degrees below the horizontal;

(ii) at least 50 percent of the required minimum intensity is maintained from 25 degrees above to 25 degrees below the horizontal.

In the case of unmanned barges the minimum required intensity of electric lights as fitted shall be maintained on the horizontal.

(c) In the case of lights other than electric these specifications shall be met as closely as possible.

11. Intensity of non-electric lights

Non-electric lights shall so far as practicable comply with the minimum intensities, as specified in the Table given in Section 8 *§84.15* of this Annex.

12. Maneuvering light

Notwithstanding the provisions of paragraph 2(f)§84.03(f) of this Annex the maneuvering light described in Rule 34(b) shall be placed in the same fore and aft vertical plane as the masthead light or lights and, where practicable, at a minimum height of 2 m *(0.5 m)* vertically above the forward masthead light, provided that it shall be carried not less than 2 m *(0.5 m)* vertically above or below the after masthead light. On a vessel where only one masthead light is carried the maneuvering light, if fitted, shall be carried where it can best be seen, not less than 2 m *(0.5 m)* vertically apart from the masthead light.

13. High-speed craft

(a) The masthead light of high-speed craft may be placed at a height related to the breadth of the craft lower than that prescribed in paragraph 2(a)(i) of this annex, provided that the base angle of the isosceles triangles formed by the sidelights and masthead light, when seen in end elevation, is not less than 27°.

(b) On high-speed craft of 50 m or more in length, the vertical separation between foremast and mainmast light of 4.5 m required by paragraph 29(a)(ii) of this annex may be modified provided that such distance shall not be less than the value determined by the following formula:

$$y = \frac{(a + 17Y)C}{1000} + 2$$

where:

+ y is the height of the mainmast light above the foremast light in m;
+ a is the height of the foremast light above the water surface in service condition in m;
+ Y is the trim in service conditions in degrees;
+ C is the horizontal separation of masthead lights in m

(a) The masthead light of high-speed craft with a length to breadth ratio of less than 3.0 may be placed at a height related to the breadth lower than that prescribed in Sec. 84.03(a)(1), provided that the base angle of the isosceles triangle formed by the sidelights and masthead light when seen in end elevation is not less than 27 degrees as determined by the formula in paragraph (b) of this section.

(b) The minimum height of masthead light above sidelights is to be determined by the following formula: Tan 27°=x/y; where Y is the horizontal distance between the sidelights and X is the height of the forward masthead light.

14. Approval *(Inland Reserved)*

The construction of lights and shapes and the installation of lights on board the vessel shall be to the satisfaction of the appropriate authority of the State whose flag the vessel is entitled to fly.

Annex II: Additional Signals for Fishing Vessels Fishing in Close Proximity

1. General

The lights mentioned herein shall, if exhibited in pursuance of Rule 26(d), be placed where they can best be seen. They shall be at least 0.9 m apart but at a lower level than lights prescribed in Rule 26(b)(i) and (c)(i). The lights shall be visible all around the horizon at a distance of at least 1 mile but at a lesser distance than the lights prescribed by these Rules for fishing vessels.

2. Signals for trawlers

(a) Vessels of 20 m or more in length *(length not mentioned in Inland)* when engaged in trawling, whether using demersal or pelagic gear, may exhibit:

   (i) when shooting their nets: two white lights in a vertical line;

   (ii) when hauling their nets: one white light over one red light in a vertical line;

   (iii) when the net has come fast upon an obstruction: two red lights in a vertical line.

(b) Each vessel of 20 meters or more in length engaged in pair trawling may exhibit *(length not given in Inland)*:

   (i) by night, a searchlight directed forward and in the direction of the other vessel of the pair;

   (ii) when shooting or hauling their nets or when their nets have come fast upon an obstruction, the lights prescribed in 2(a) above.

3. Signals for purse seiners

Vessels engaged in fishing with purse seine gear may exhibit two yellow lights in a vertical line. These lights shall flash alternately every second and with equal light and occultation duration. These lights may be exhibited only when the vessel is hampered by its fishing gear.

Annex III: Technical Details of Sound Signal Appliances

1. Whistles

(a) **Frequencies and range of audibility.** The fundamental frequency of the signal shall lie within the range 70-700 Hz *(70-525 Hz)*. The range of audibility of the signal from a whistle shall be determined by those frequencies, which may include the fundamental and/or one or more higher frequencies, which lie within the range 180-700 Hz ($\pm$1%) for a vessel of 20 meters or more in length, or 180-2100Hz ($\pm$1%) for a vessel of less than 20 meters in length and which provide the sound pressure levels specified in paragraph 1(c) *§86.05* below.

(b) **Limits of fundamental frequencies.** To ensure a wide variety of whistle characteristics, the fundamental frequency of a whistle shall be between the following limits:

(i) 70-200 Hz, for a vessel 200 m or more in length;

(ii) 130-350 Hz, for a vessel 75 m but <200 m in length;

(iii) 250-700 Hz *(250-525 Hz)*, for a vessel <75 m in length.

(c) **Sound signal intensity and range of audibility.** A whistle fitted in a vessel shall provide, in the direction of maximum intensity of the whistle and at a distance of 1 meter from it, a sound pressure level in at least one 1/3-octave band within the range of frequencies 180-700 Hz ($\pm$1%) for a vessel of 20 meters or more in length, or 180-2100Hz ($\pm$1%) for a vessel of less than 20 meters in length, of not less than the appropriate figure given in the table below.

Length of vessel, m	⅓ octave band level at 1m in dB referred to 2 x 10^{-5} N/m^2	Audibility range, nm
200 or more	143	2
75 but less than 200	138	1.5
20 but less than 75	130	1
Less than 20	120[1]	0.5
	115[2]	
	111[3]	

1 When the measured frequencies lie within the range 180-450Hz

2 When the measured frequencies lie within the range 450-800Hz

3 When the measured frequencies lie within the range 800-2100Hz

§ 86.05 Sound signal intensity and range of audibility.

A whistle on a vessel shall provide, in the direction of the forward axis of the whistle and at a distance of 1 meter from it, a sound pressure level in at least one ⅓ octave band of not less than the appropriate figure given in Table 86.05 within the following frequency ranges (±1 percent):

(a) 130-1200 Hz, for a vessel 75 m or more in length;
(b) 250-1600 Hz, for a vessel 20 m but < 75 m in length;
(c) 250-2100 Hz, for a vessel 12 m but < 20 m in length.

Table 86.05

Length of vessel in meters	Fundamental frequency range (Hz)	For measured frequencies (Hz)	⅓ octave band level at 1 meter in dB referred to 2×10^{-5} N/m²	Audibility range in nautical miles
200 or more	70-200	130-180	145	2
		180-250	143	
		250-1200	140	
75 but <200	130-350	130-180	140	1.5
		180-250	138	
		250-1200	134	
20 but <75	250-525	250-450	130	1.0
		450-800	125	
		800-1600	121	
12 but <20	250-525	250-450	120	0.5
		450-800	115	
		800-2100	111	

NOTE: The range of audibility in the table above is for information and is approximately the range at which a whistle may be heard on its forward axis with 90 percent probability in conditions of still air on board a vessel having average background noise level at the listening posts (taken to be 68 dB in the octave band centered on 250 Hz and 63 dB in the octave band centered on 500 Hz). In practice the range at which a whistle may be heard is extremely variable and depends critically on weather conditions; the values given can be regarded as typical but under conditions of strong wind or high ambient noise level at the listening post the range may be much reduced.

(d) *§86.07* **Directional Properties.** The sound pressure level of a directional whistle shall be not more than 4 dB below the prescribed sound pressure level on that axis at any direction in the horizontal plane within ±45 degrees of the axis. The sound pressure level at any other direction in the horizontal plane shall be not more than 10 dB below the prescribed sound pressure level on the axis, so that the range in any direction will be at least half the range on the forward axis. The sound pressure level shall be measured in that one-third octave band which determines the audibility range.

(e) *§86.09* **Positioning of whistles.** When a directional whistle is to be used as the only whistle on a vessel, it shall be installed with its maximum intensity directed straight ahead. A whistle shall be placed as high as practicable on a vessel, in order to reduce interception of the emitted sound by obstructions and also to minimize hearing damage risk to personnel. The sound pressure level of the vessel's own signal at listening posts shall not exceed 110 dB (A) and so far as practicable should not exceed 100 dB (A).

(f) *§86.11* **Fitting of more than one whistle.** If whistles are fitted at a distance apart of no more than 100 m, it shall be so arranged that they are not sounded simultaneously.

(g) *§86.13* **Combined whistle systems.** If due to the presence of obstructions the sound field of a single whistle or of one of the whistles referred to in paragraph 1(f) above is likely to have a zone of greatly reduced signal level, it is recommended that a combined whistle system be fitted so as to overcome this reduction. For the purposes of the Rules a combined whistle system is to be regarded as a single whistle. The whistles of a combined system shall be located at a distance apart of not more than 100 m and arranged to be sounded simultaneously. The frequency of any one whistle shall differ from those of the others by at least 10 Hz (100 Hz).

§86.13 Combined whistle systems

(a) A combined whistle system is a number of whistles (sound emitting sources) operated together. For the purposes of the Rules a combined whistle system is to be regarded as a single whistle.

(b) The whistles of a combined system shall:

(1) Be located at a distance apart of not more than 100 meters,

(2) Be sounded simultaneously,

(3) Each have a fundamental frequency different from those of the others by at least 10 Hz, and

(4) Have a tonal characteristic appropriate for the length of vessel which shall be evidenced by at least two-thirds of the whistles in the combined system having fundamental frequencies falling within the limits prescribed in §86.03, or if there are only two whistles in the combined system, by the higher fundamental frequency falling within the limits prescribed in §86.03.

NOTE: If due to the presence of obstructions the sound field of a single whistle or of one of the whistles referred to in §86.11 is likely to have a zone of greatly reduced signal level a combined whistle system should be fitted so as to overcome this reduction.

§86.15 **Towing vessel whistles.** *A power-driven vessel normaly engaged in pushing ahead or towing alongside may, at all times, use a whistle whose characteristic falls within the limits prescribed by §86.03 for the longest customary composite length of the vessel and its tow.*

2. Bell or gong

(a) *§86.21* **Intensity of signal.** A bell or gong, or other device having similar sound characteristics shall produce a sound pressure level of not less than 110 dB at a distance of 1 m from it.

(b) *§86.23* **Construction.** Bells and gongs shall be made of corrosion-resistant material and be designed to give a clear tone. The diameter of the mouth of the bell shall be no less than 300 mm for vessels of 20 m or more in length *(and shall not be less than 200 mm for vesssels 12 to 20 m in length)*. Where practicable, a power-driven bell striker is recommended to ensure constant force but manual operation shall be possible. The mass of the striker shall be not less than 3 percent of the mass of the bell. *The striker shall be capable of manual operation.*

3. Approval (International only)

The construction of sound signal appliances, their performance and their installation on board the vessel shall be to the satisfaction of the appropriate authority of the State whose flag the vessel is entitled to fly.

Annex IV: Distress Signals

1. The following signals, used or exhibited together or separately, indicate distress and need of assistance (see page 41).

(a) a gun or other explosive signal fired at intervals of about a minute;

(b) a continuous sounding with any fog-signalling apparatus;

(c) rockets or shells, throwing red stars fired one at a time at short intervals;

(d) a signal made by radiotelegraphy or by any other signaling method consisting of the group . . . − − − . . . (SOS) in the Morse Code;

(e) a signal sent by radiotelephony consisting of the spoken word "Mayday";

(f) the International Code Signal of distress indicated by N.C.;

(g) a signal consisting of a square flag having above or below it a ball or anything resembling a ball;

(h) flames on the vessel (as from a burning tar barrel, oil barrel, etc.);

(i) a rocket parachute flare or a hand flare showing a red light;

(j) a smoke signal giving off orange-colored smoke;

(k) slowly and repeatedly raising and lowering arms outstretched to each side;

(l) the radiotelegraph alarm signal;

(m) the radiotelephone alarm signal;

(n) signals transmitted by emergency position-indicating radio beacons.

(o) approved signals transmitted by radiocommunication systems, including survival craft radar transponders.

(p) A high intensity white light flashing at regular intervals from 50 to 70 times per minute.

2. *§87.3* The use or exhibition of any of the foregoing signals except for the purpose of indicating distress and need of assistance and the use of other signals which may be confused with any of the above signals is prohibited.

3. *§87.5* Attention is drawn to the relevant sections of the International Code of Signals, the Merchant Ship Search and Rescue Manual and the following signals: (a) a piece of orange-colored canvas with either a black square and circle or other appropriate symbol (for identification from the air); (b) a dye marker.

Annex V: Pilot Rules (Inland Only)

§88.01 *Purpose and applicability.*

This part applies to all vessels operating on United States Inland waters and to United States vessels operating on the Canadian waters of the Great Lakes to the extent there is no conflict with Canadian law.

§88.03 *Definitions.*

The terms used in this part have the same meaning as defined in the Inland Navigational Rules Act of 1980.

§88.05 *Copy of Rules.*

After January 1, 1983, the operator of each self-propelled vessel 12 m or more in length shall carry on board and maintain for ready reference a copy of the Inland Navigation Rules.

§88.09 *Temporary exemption from light and shape requirements when operating under bridges.*

A vessel's navigation lights and shapes may be lowered if necessary to pass under a bridge.

§88.11 *Law enforcement vessels.*

(a) Law enforcement vessels may display a flashing blue light when engaged in direct law enforcement activities. This light shall be located so that it does not interfere with the visibility of the vessel's navigation lights.

(b) The blue light described in this section may be displayed by law enforcement vessels of the United States and the States and their political subdivisions.

§88.12 *Public Safety Activities.*

(a) Vessels engaged in government sanctioned public safety activities, and commercial vessels performing similar functions, may display an alternately flashing red and yellow light signal. This identification light signal must be located so that it does not interfere with the visibility of the vessel's navigation lights. The identification light signal may be used only as an identification signal and conveys no special privilege. Vessels using the identification light signal during public safety activities must abide by the Inland Navigation Rules, and must not presume that the light or the exigency gives them precedence or right of way.

(b) Public safety activities include but are not limited to patrolling marine parades, regattas, or special water celebrations; traffic control; salvage; fire-fighting; medical assistance; assisting disabled vessels; and search and rescue.

§ 88.13 *Lights on moored barges.*

(a) The following barges shall display at night and if practicable in periods of restricted visibility the lights described in paragraph (b) of this section:

    (1) Every barge projecting into a buoyed or restricted channel.

    (2) Every barge so moored that it reduces the available navigable width of any channel to less than 80 meters.

(3) *Barges moored in groups more than two barges wide or to a maximum width of over 25 meters.*

(4) *Every barge not moored parallel to the bank or dock.*

(b) *Barges described in paragraph (a) of this section shall carry two unobstructed all-round white lights of an intensity to be visible for at least one nautical mile and meeting the technical requirements as prescribed in §84.15 of this chapter.*

(c) *A barge or a group of barges at anchor or made fast to one or more mooring bouys or other similar device, in lieu of the provisions of Inland Navigation Rule 30, may carry unobstructed all-round white lights of an intensity to be visible for at least one nautical mile that meet the requirements of §84.15 of this chapter and shall be arranged as follows:*

(1) *Any barge that projects from a group formation, shall be lighted on its outboard corners.*

(2) *On a single barge moored in water where other vessels normally navigate on both sides of the barge, lights shall be placed to mark the corner extremities of the barge.*

(3) *On barges moored in group formation, moored in water where other vessels normally navigate on both sides of the group, lights shall be placed to mark the corner extremities of the group.*

(d) *The following are exempt from the requirements of this section:*

(1) *A barge or group of barges moored in a slip or slough used primarily for mooring purposes.*

(2) *A barge or group of barges moored behind a pierhead.*

(3) *A barge less than 20 meters in length when moored in a special anchorage area designated in accordance with §109.10 of this chapter.*

(e) *Barges moored in well-illuminated areas are exempt from the lighting requirements of this section. These areas are as follows:*

§88.15 **Lights on dredge pipelines.**

Chicago Sanitary Ship Canal

(1) *Mile 293.2 to 293.9*

(3) *Mile 295.2 to 296.1*

(5) *Mile 297.5 to 297.8*

(7) *Mile 298 to 298.2*

(9) *Mile 298.6 to 298.8*

(11) *Mile 299.3 to 299.4*

(13) *Mile 299.8 to 300.5*

(15) *Mile 303 to 303.2*

(17) *Mile 303.7 to 303.9*

(21) *Mile 310.7 to 310.9*

(23) *Mile 311 to 311.2*

(25) *Mile 312.5 to 312.6*

(27) *Mile 313.8 to 314.2*

(29) *Mile 314.6*

(31) *Mile 314.8 to 315.3*

(33) *Mite 315.7 to 316*

(35) *Mile 316.8*

(37) *Mile 316.85 to 317.05*

(39) *Mile 317.5*

(41) *Mile 318.4 to 318.9*

(43) *Mile 318.7 to 318.8*

(45) *Mile 320 to 320.3*

(47) *Mile 320.6*

(49) *Mile 322.3 to 322.4*

(51) *Mile 322.8*

(53) *Mile 322.9 to 327.2*

Calumet Sag Channel

(61) Mile 316.5

Little Calumet River

(71) Mile 321,2

(73) Mile 322.3

Calumet River

(81) Mile 328.5 to 328.7

(83) Mile 329.2 to 329.4

(85) Mile 330, West bank to 330.2

(87) Mile 331.4 to 331.6

(89) Mile 332.2 to 332.4

(91) Mile 332.6 to 332.8

Cumberland River

(101) Mile 126.8

(103) Mile 191

Dredge pipelines that are floating or supported on trestles shall display the following lights at night and in periods of restricted visibility.

(a) One row of yellow lights. The lights must be—

> *(1) Flashing 50 to 70 times per minute,*

> *(2) Visible all around the horizon,*

> *(3) Visible for at least 2 miles on a clear dark night,*

> *(4) Not less than 1 and not more than 3.5 m above the water,*

> *(5) Approximately equally spaced, and*

> *(6) Not more than 10 m apart where the pipeline crosses a navigable channel. Where the pipeline does not cross a navigable channel the lights must be sufficient in number to clearly show the pipeline's length and course.*

(b) Two red lights at each end of the pipeline, including the ends in a channel where the pipeline is separated to allow vessels to pass (whether open or closed). The lights must be—

> *(1) Visible all around the horizon, and*

> *(2) Visible for at least 2 miles on a clear dark night, and*

> *(3) One m apart in a vertical line with the lower light at the same height above the water as the flashing yellow light.*

— INTERPRETATIVE RULES —

§82.1 **Purpose.**

(a) This part contains the interpretative rules concerning the 72 COLREGS that are adopted by the CG for the guidance of the public.

§90.1 (a) This part contains the interpretative rules for the Inland Rules. These interpretative rules are intended as a guide to assist the public and promote compliance with the Inland Rules.

§82.3 **Pushing vessel and vessel being pushed: Composite unit.**

Rule 24(b) of the 72 COLREGS states that when a pushing vessel and a vessel being pushed ahead are rigidly connected in a composite unit, they are regarded as a power-driven vessel and must exhibit the lights under Rule 23. A "composite unit" is interpreted to be a pushing vessel that is rigidly connected by mechanical means to a vessel being pushed so they react to sea and swell as one vessel. "Mechanical means" does not include the following: (a) Lines. (b) Hawsers. (c) Wires. (d) Chains.

§82.5 **Lights for moored vessels**

For the purposes of Rule 30 of the 72 COLREGS, a vessel at anchor includes a barge made fast to one or more mooring buoys or other similar device attached to the sea or river floor. Such a barge may be lighted as a vessel at anchor in accordance with Rule 30, or may be lighted on the corners in accordance with 33 CFR 88.13.

§90.5 Lights for moored vessels

A vessel at anchor includes a vessel made fast to one or more mooring buoys or other similar device attached to the ocean floor. Such vessels may be lighted as a vessel at anchor in accordance with Rule 30, or may be lighted on the corners in accordance with 33 CFR 88.13.

§82.7 **Sidelights for unmanned barges**

An unmanned barge being towed may use the exception of COLREG Rule 24(h). However, this exception only applies to the vertical sector requirements.

§90.7 Sidelights for unmanned barges

An unmanned barge being towed may use the exception of COLREG Rule 24(h). However, this exception only applies to the vertical sector requirements.

COLREGS Demarcation Lines

General
80.01 General basis and purpose of demarcation lines.

ATLANTIC COAST
FIRST DISTRICT
80.105 Calais, ME to Cape Small, ME.

80.110 Casco Bay, ME.

80.115 Portland Head, ME to Cape Ann, MA.

80.120 Cape Ann, MA to Marblehead Neck, MA.

80.125 Marblehead Neck, MA to Nahant, MA.

80.130 Boston Harbor entrance.

80.135 Hull, MA to Race Point, MA.

80.145 Race Point, MA to Watch Hill, RI.

80.150 Block Island, RI.

80.155 Watch Hill, RI to Montauk Point, NY.

80.160 Montauk Point, NY to Atlantic Beach, NY.

80.165 New York Harbor.

80.170 Sandy Hook, NJ to Tom's River, NJ.

FIFTH DISTRICT
80.501 Tom's River NJ, to Cape May, NJ

80.503 Delaware Bay.

80.505 Cape Henlopen, DE to Cape Charles, VA.

80.510 Chesapeake Bay Entrance, VA.

80.520 Cape Hatteras, NC to Cape Lookout, NC.

80.525 Cape Lookout, NC to Cape Fear, NC.

80.530 Cape Fear, NC to New River Inlet, NC.

SEVENTH DISTRICT
80.703 Little River Inlet, SC to Cape Romain, SC.

80.707 Cape Romain, SC to Sullivans Island, SC.

80.710 Charleston Harbor, SC.

80.712 Morris Island, SC to Hilton Head Island, SC.

80.715 Savannah River.

80.717 Tybee Island, GA to St. Simons Island, GA.

80.720 St. Simons Island, GA to Amelia Island, FL.

80.723 Amelia Island, FL to Cape Canaveral, FL.

80.727 Cape Canaveral, FL to Miami Beach, FL.

80.730 Miami Harbor, FL.

80.735 Miami, FL to Long Key, FL.

PUERTO RICO AND VIRGIN ISLANDS
SEVENTH DISTRICT
80.738 Puerto Rico and Virgin Islands.

GULF COAST
SEVENTH DISTRICT
80.740 Long Key, FL to Cape Sable, FL.

80.745 Cape Sable, FL to Cape Romano, FL.

80.748 Cape Romano, FL to Sanibel Island, FL.

80.750 Sanibel Island, FL to St. Petersburg, FL.

80.753 St. Petersburg, FL to Anclote, FL.

80.755 Anclote, FL to the Suncoast Keys, FL.

80.757 Suncoast Keys, FL to Horseshoe Point, FL

80.760 Horseshoe Point, FL to Rock Island, FL.

EIGHTH DISTRICT
80.805 Rock Island, FL to Cape San Blas, FL.

80.810 Cape San Blas, FL to Perdido Bay, FL.

80.815 Mobile Bay, AL to the Chandeleur Island, LA.

80.825 Mississippi Passes, LA.

80.830 Mississippi Passes, LA to Point Au Fer, LA.

80.835 Point Au Fer, LA to Calcasieu Pass, LA.

80.840 Sabine Pass, TX to Galveston, TX.

80.845 Galveston, TX to Freeport, TX.

80.850 Brazos River, TX to the Rio Grande, TX.

PACIFIC COAST

ELEVENTH DISTRICT

80.1105 Santa Catalina Island, CA.

80.1110 San Diego Harbor, CA.

80.1115 Mission Bay, CA.

80.1120 Oceanside Harbor, CA.

80.1125 Dana Point Harbor, CA.

80.1130 Newport Bay, CA.

80.1135 San Pedro Bay—Anaheim Bay, CA.

80.1140 Redondo Harbor, CA.

80.1145 Marina Del Rey, CA.

80.1150 Port Hueneme, CA.

80.1155 Channel Islands Harbor, CA.

TWELFTH DISTRICT

80.1205 San Luis Obispo Bay, CA.

80.1210 Estero—Morro Bay, CA.

80.1215 Monterey Harbor, CA.

80.1220 Moss Landing Harbor, CA.

80.1225 Santa Cruz Harbor, CA.

80.1230 Pillar Point Harbor, CA.

80.1250 San Francisco Harbor, CA.

80.1255 Bodega and Tomales Bay, CA.

80.1260 Albion River, CA.

80.1265 Noyo River, CA.

80.1270 Arcato—Humboldt Bay, CA.

80.1275 Crescent City Harbor, CA.

THIRTEENTH DISTRICT

80.1305 Chetco River, OR.

80.1310 Rogue River, OR.

80.1315 Coquille River, OR.

80.1320 Coos Bay, OR.

80.1325 Umpqua River, OR.

80.1330 Sinslaw River, OR.

80.1335 Alsea Bay, OR.

80.1340 Yaquina Bay, OR.

80.1345 Depoe Bay, OR.

80.1350 Netarts Bay, OR.

80.1355 Tillamook Bay, OR.

80.1360 Nehalem River, OR.

80.1365 Columbia River Entrance, OR/WA.

80.1370 Willapa Bay, WA.

80.1375 Grays Harbor, WA.

80.1380 Quillayute River.

80.1385 Strait of Juan de Fuca.

80.1390 Haro Strait and Strait of Georgia.

80.1395 Puget Sound and Adjacent Waters.

PACIFIC ISLANDS

FOURTEENTH DISTRICT

80.1410 Hawaiian Island Exemption from General rule.

80.1420 Mamala Bay, Oahu, HI.

80.1430 Kaneohe Bay, Oahu, HI.

80.1 440 Port Allen, Kauai, HI.

80.1450 Nawiliwili Harbor, Kauai, HI.

80.1460 Kahului Harbor, Maui, HI.

80.1470 Kawaihae Harbor, Hawaii, HI.

80.1480 Hilo Harbor, Hawaii, HI.

80.1490 Apra Harbor, U.S. Territory of Guam.

80.1495 U.S. Pacific Island Possessions.

ALASKA

SEVENTEENTH DISTRICT

1705 Alaska.

AUTHORITY:

Rule 1, International Regulations for Preventing Collisions at Sea, 1972 (as rectified); E.O. 11964; Pub. L. 95-75, 91 Stat. 308; 14 U.S.C. 2;49 CFR 1.46(b), unless otherwise noted. SOURCE: CGD 77-118a, 42 FR 35784, July 11, 1977, unless otherwise noted.

GENERAL

§80.01 General basis and purpose of demarcation lines.

(a) The regulations in this part establish the lines of demarcation delineating those waters upon which mariners shall comply with the International Regulations for Preventing Collisions at Sea, 1972 (72 COLREGS) and those waters upon which mariners shall comply with the Inland Navigation Rules.

(b) The waters inside of the lines are Inland Rules Waters. The waters outside the lines are COLREGS Waters.

ATLANTIC COAST

FIRST DISTRICT

§80.105 Calais, ME to Cape Small, ME.

The 72 COLREGS shall apply on the harbors, bays, and inlets on the east coast of Maine from International Bridge at Calais, ME to the southwesternmost extremity of Bald Head at Cape Small.

§80.110 Casco Bay, ME.

(a) A line drawn from the southwesternmost extremity of Bald Head at Cape Small to the southeasternmost extremity of Ragged Island; thence to the southern tangent of Jaquish Island thence to Little Mark Island Monument Light; thence to the northernmost extremity of Jewell Island.

(b) A line drawn from the tower on Jewell Island charted in approximate position latitude 43°40.6' N. longitude 70°05.9' W. to the northeasternmost extremity of Outer Green Island.

(c) A line drawn from the southwesternmost extremity of Outer Green Island to Ram Island Ledge Light; thence to Portland Head Light.

§80.115 Portland Head, ME to Cape Ann, MA.

(a) Except inside lines specifically described in this section, the 72 COLREGS shall apply on the harbors, bays, and inlets on the east coast of Maine, New Hampshire, and Massachusetts from Portland Head to Halibut Point at Cape Ann.

(b) A line drawn from the southernmost tower on Gerrish Island charted in approximate position latitude 43°04.0 N. longitude 70°41.2' W. to Whaleback Light; thence to Jeffrey Point Light 2A; thence to the northeasternmost extremity of Frost Point.

(c) A line drawn from the northernmost extremity of Farm Point to Annisquam Harbor Light.

§80.120 Cape Ann, MA to Marblehead Neck, MA.

(a) Except inside lines specifically described in this section, the 72 COLREGS shall apply on the harbors, bays and inlets on the east coast of Massachusetts from Halibut Point at Cape Ann to Marblehead Neck.

(b) A line drawn from Gloucester Harbor Breakwater Light to the twin towers charted in approximate position latitude 42°35.1'N. longitude 70°41.6'W.

(c) A line drawn from the westernmost extremity of Gales Point to the easternmost extremity of House Island; thence to Bakers Island Light; thence to Marblehead Light.

§80.125 Marblehead Neck, MA to Nahant, MA.

The 72 COLREGS apply on the harbors, bays, and inlets on the east coast of Massachusetts from Marblehead Neck to the easternmost tower at Nahant, charted in approximate position latitude 42°25.4'N., longitude 70°54.6'W.

§80.130 Boston Harbor entrance.

A line drawn from eastern most tower at Nahant, charted in approximate position latitude 42°25.4'N., longitude 70°54.6'W., to Boston Lighted Horn Buoy "B"; thence to the eastern most radio tower at Hull, charted in approximate position latitude 42°16.7'N., longitude 70°52.6'W.

§80.135 Hull, MA to Race Point, MA.

(a) Except inside lines described in this section, the 72 COLREGS apply on the harbors, bays, and inlets on the east coast of Massachusetts from the easternmost radio tower at Hull, charted in approximate position latitude 42°16.7'N., longitude 70°52.6'W., to Race Point on Cape Cod.

(b) A line drawn from Canal Breakwater Light 4 south to the shoreline.

§80.145 Race Point, MA to Watch Hill, RI.

(a) Except inside lines specifically described in this section, the 72 COLREGS shall apply on the sounds, bays, harbors and inlets along the coast of Cape Cod and the southern coasts of Massachusetts and Rhode Island from Race Point to Watch Hill.

(b) A line drawn from Nobska Point Light to Tarpaulin Cove Light on the southeastern side of Naushon Island; thence from the southernmost tangent of Naushon Island to the easternmost extremity of Nashawena Island; thence from the southwestern most extremity of Nashawena Island to the easternmost extremity of Cuttyhunk Island; thence from the southwestern tangent of Cuttyhunk Island to the tower on Gooseberry Neck charted in approximate position latitude 41°29.1'N. longitude 71°02.3'W.

(c) A line drawn from Sakonnet Breakwater Light 2 tangent to the southernmost part of Sacnuest Point charted in approximate position latitude 41°28.5'N. longitude 71°14.8'W.

(d) An east-west line drawn through Beavertail Light between Brenton Point and the Boston Neck shoreline.

§80.150 Block Island, RI.

The 72 COLREGS shall apply on the harbors of Block Island.

§80.155 Watch Hill, RI to Montauk Point, NY.

(a) A line drawn from Watch Hill Light to East Point on Fishers Island.

(b) A line drawn from Race Point to Race Rock Light; thence to Little Gull Island Light thence to East Point on Plum Island.

(c) A line drawn from Plum Island Harbor East Dolphin Light to Plum Island Harbor West Dolphin Light.

(d) A line drawn from Plum Island Light to Orient Point Light; thence to Orient Point.

(e) A line drawn from the lighthouse ruins at the southwestern end of Long Beach Point to Cornelius Point.

(f) A line drawn from Coecles Harbor Entrance Light to Sungic Point.

(g) A line drawn from Nichols Point to Cedar Island Light.

(h) A line drawn from Three Mile Harbor West Breakwater Light to Three Mile Harbor East Breakwater Light.

(i) A line drawn from Montauk West Jetty Light 1 to Montauk East Jetty Light 2.

§80.160 Montauk Point, NY to Atlantic Beach, NY.

(a) A line drawn from Shinnecock Inlet East Breakwater Light to Shinnecock Inlet West Breakwater Light 1.

(b) A line drawn from Moriches Inlet East Breakwater Light to Moriches Inlet West Breakwater Light.

(c) A line drawn from Fire Island Inlet Breakwater Light 348° true to the southernmost extremity of the spit of land at the western end of Oak Beach.

(d) A line drawn from Jones Inlet Light 322° true across the southwest tangent of the island on the north side of Jones Inlet to the shoreline.

§80.165 New York Harbor.

A line drawn from East Rockaway Inlet Breakwater Light to Sandy Hook Light.

§80.170 Sandy Hook, NJ to Tom's River, NJ.

(a) A line drawn from Shark River Inlet North Breakwater Light 2 to Shark River Inlet South Breakwater Light 1.

(b) A line drawn from Manasquan Inlet North Breakwater Light 4 to Manasquan Inlet South Breakwater Light 3.

(c) A line drawn from Barnegat Inlet North Breakwater Light 4A to the seaward extremity of the submerged Barnegat Inlet South Breakwater; thence along the submerged breakwater to the shoreline.

FIFTH DISTRICT

§80.501 Tom's River, NJ to Cape May, NJ

(a) A line drawn from the seaward tangent of Long Beach Island to the seaward tangent to Pullen Island across Beach Haven and Little Egg Inlets.

(b) A line drawn from the seaward tangent of Pullen Island to the seaward tangent of Brigantine Island across Brigantine Inlet.

(c) A line drawn from the seaward extremity of Absecon Inlet North Jetty to Atlantic City Light.

(d) A line drawn from the southernmost point of Longport at latitude 30°18.2'N longitude 75°32.2'W. to the northeasternmost point of Ocean City at latitude 39°17.6'N. longitude 74°33.1' W. across Great Egg Harbor Inlet.

(e) A line drawn parallel with the general trend of highwater shoreline across Corson Inlet.

(f) A line formed by the centerline of the Townsend Inlet Highway Bridge.

(g) A line formed by the shoreline of Seven Mile Beach and Hereford Inlet Light.

(h) A line drawn from Cape May Inlet West Jetty Light.

§80.503 Delaware Bay.

A line drawn from Cape May Light to Harbor of Refuge Light; thence to the northernmost extremity of Cape Henlopen.

§80.505 Cape Henlopen, DE to Cape Charles, VA.

(a) A line drawn from the seaward extremity of Indian River Inlet North Jetty to Indian River Inlet South Jetty Light.

(b) A line drawn from Ocean City Inlet Light 6 225° true across Ocean City Inlet to the submerged south breakwater.

(c) A line drawn from Assateague Beach Tower Light to the tower charted at latitude 37°52.6'N. longitude 75°26.7'W.

(d) A line formed by the range of Wachapreague Inlet Light 3 and Parramore Beach Lookout Tower drawn across Wachapreague Inlet.

(e) A line drawn from the lookout tower charted on the northern end of Hog Island to the seaward tangent of Parramore Beach.

(f) A line drawn 207° true from the lookout tower charted on the southern end of Hog Island across Great Machipongo Inlet.

(g) A line formed by the range of the two cupolas charted on the southern end of Cobb Island drawn across Sand Shoal Inlet.

(h) Except as provided elsewhere in this section from Cape Henlopen to Cape Charles, lines drawn parallel with the general trend of the highwater shoreline across the entrances to small bays and inlets.

§80.510 Chesapeake Bay Entrance, VA.

A line drawn from Cape Charles Light to Cape Henry Light.

§80.515 Cape Henry, VA to Cape Hatteras, NC.

(a) A line drawn from Rudee Inlet Jetty Light 2 to Rudee Inlet Jetty Light 1.

(b) A line formed by the centerline of the highway bridge across Oregon Inlet.

§80.520 Cape Hatteras, NC to Cape Lookout, NC.

(a) A line drawn from Hatteras Inlet Lookout Tower (30° 11.8'N 75° 44.9'W) 255° true to the eastern end of Ocracoke Island.

(b) A line drawn from the westernmost extremity of Ocracoke Island at latitude 35° 04.0'N. longitude 76° 00.8'W. to the northeastern extremity of Portsmouth Island at latitude 35° 03.7'N. longitude 76° 02.3'W.

(c) A line drawn across Drum Inlet parallel with the general trend of the highwater shoreline.

§80.525 Cape Lookout, NC to Cape Fear, NC.

(a) A line drawn from Cape Lookout Light to the seaward tangent of the southeastern end of Shackleford Banks.

(b) A line drawn from Morehead City Channel Range Front Light to the seaward extremity of the Beaufort Inlet west jetty.

(c) A line drawn from the southernmost extremity of Bogue Banks at latitude 34° 38.7'N. longitude 77° 06.0'W. across Bogue Inlet to the northernmost extremity of Bear Beach at latitude 34° 38.5'N. longitude 77° 07.1'W.

(d) A line drawn from the tower charted in approximate position latitude 34° 31.5'N. longitude 77° 20.8'W to the seaward tangent of the shoreline on the northeast side of New River Inlet.

(e) A line drawn across New Topsail Inlet between the closest extremities of the shore on either side of the inlet from latitude 34° 20.8'N. longitude 77° 39.2'W. to latitude 34° 20.6' N. longitude 77° 39.6'W.

(f) A line drawn from the seaward extremity of the jetty on the northeast side of Masonboro Inlet to the seaward extremity of the jetty on the southeast side of the Inlet.

(g) Except as provided elsewhere in this section from Cape Lookout to Cape Fear, lines drawn parallel with the general trend of the highwater shoreline across the entrance of small bays and inlets.

§80.530 Cape Fear, NC to Little River Inlet, NC.

(a) A line drawn from the abandoned lighthouse charted in approximate position latitude 33° 52.4'N. longitude 78° 00.1'W. across the Cape Fear River Entrance to Oak Island Light.

(b) Except as provided elsewhere in this section from Cape Fear to Little River Inlet, lines drawn parallel with the general trend of the highwater shoreline across the entrance to small inlets.

SEVENTH DISTRICT

§80.703 Little River Inlet, SC to Cape Romain, SC.

(a) A line drawn from the westernmost extremity of the sand spit on Bird Island to the easternmost extremity of Waties Island across Little River Inlet.

(b) From Little River Inlet, a line drawn parallel with the general trend of the highwater shoreline across Hog Inlet; thence a line drawn from Murrels Inlet Light 2 to Murrels Inlet Light 1;

thence a line drawn parallel with the general trend of the highwater shoreline across Midway Inlet, Pawleys Inlet and North Inlet.

(c) A line drawn from the charted position of Winyah Bay North Jetty End Buoy 2N south to the Winyah Bay South Jetty.

(d) A line drawn from Santee Point to the seaward tangent of Cedar Island.

(e) A line drawn from Cedar Island Point west to Murphy Island.

(f) A north-south line (longitude 79° 20.3'W.) drawn from Murphy Island to the northernmost extremity of Cape Island Point.

§80.707 Cape Romain, SC to Sullivans Island, SC.

(a) A line drawn from the western extremity of Cape Romain 292° true to Racoon Key on the west side of Racoon Creek.

(b) A line drawn from the westernmost extremity of Sandy Point across Bull Bay to the northernmost extremity of Northeast Point.

(c) A line drawn from the southernmost extremity of Bull Island to the easternmost extremity of Capers Island.

(d) A line formed by the overhead power cable from Capers Island to Dewees Island.

(e) A line formed by the overhead power cable from Dewees Island to Isle of Palms.

(f) A line formed by the centerline of the highway bridge between Isle of Palms and Sullivans Island over Breach Inlet.

§80.710 Charleston Harbor, SC.

(a) A line formed by the submerged north jetty from the shore to the west end of the north jetty.

(b) A line drawn from across the seaward extremity of the Charleston Harbor Jetties.

(c) A line drawn from the west end of the South Jetty across the South Entrance to Charleston Harbor to shore on a line formed by the submerged south jetty.

§80.712 Morris Island, SC to Hilton Head Island, SC.

(a) A line drawn from the easternmost tip of Folley Island to the abandoned lighthouse tower on the north side of Lighthouse Inlet; thence west to the shoreline of Morris Island.

(b) A straight line drawn from the seaward tangent of Folly Island through Folly River Daybeacon 10 across Stono River to the shoreline of Sandy Point.

(c) A line drawn from the southernmost extremity of Seabrook Island 257° true across the North Edisto River Entrance to the shore of Botany Bay Island.

(d) A line drawn from the microwave antenna tower on Edisto Beach charted in approximate position latitude 32° 29.3' N. longitude 80° 19.2'W. across St. Helena Sound to the abandoned lighthouse tower on Hunting Island.

(e) A line formed by the centerline of the highway bridge between Hunting Island and Fripp Island.

(f) A line following the general trend of the seaward highwater shoreline across Cabretta Inlet.

§80.715 Savannah River.

A line drawn from the southernmost tank on Hilton Head Island charted in approximate position latitude 32° 06.7'N. longitude 80° 49.3'W. to Bloody Point Range Rear Light; thence to Tybee (Range Rear) Light.

§80.717 Tybee Island, GA to St. Simons Island, GA.

(a) A line drawn from the southernmost extremity of Savannah Beach on Tybee Island 255° true across Tybee Inlet to the shore of Little Tybee Island south of the entrance to Buck Hammock Creek.

(b) A straight line drawn from the northernmost extremity of Wassaw Island 031° true through Tybee River Daybeacon 1 to the shore of Little Tybee Island.

(c) A line drawn approximately parallel with the general trend of the highwater shorelines from the seaward tangent of Wassau Island to the seaward tangent of Bradley Point on Ossabaw Island.

(d) A north-south line (longitude 81° 08.4'W.) drawn from the southernmost extremity of Ossabaw Island to St. Catherines Island.

(e) A north-south line (longitude 81° 10.6'W.) drawn from the southernmost extremity of St. Catherines Island to Northeast Point on Blackbeard Island.

(f) A line following the general trend of the seaward highwater shoreline across Cabretta Inlet.

(g) A north-south line (longitude 81° 16.9'W.) drawn from the southwesternmost point on Sapelo Island to Wolf Island.

(h) A north-south line (longitude 81° 17.1'W.) drawn from the southeasternmost point of Wolf Island to the northeasternmost point on Little St. Simons Island.

(i) A line drawn from the northeasternmost extremity of Sea Island 045° true to Little St. Simons Island.

(j) An east-west line from the southernmost extremity of Sea Island across Goulds Inlet to St. Simons Island.

§80.720 St. Simons Island, GA to Amelia Island, FL.

(a) A line drawn from St. Simons Light to the northernmost tank on Jekyll Island charted in approximate position latitude 31° 05.9'N. longitude 81° 24.5'W.

(b) A line drawn from the southernmost tank on Jekyll Island charted in approximate position latitude 31° 01.6'N. longitude 81° 25.2'W. to coordinate latitude 30° 59.4'N. longitude 81° 23.7' W. (0.5 nautical mile east of the charted position of St. Andrew Sound Lighted Buoy 32); thence to the abandoned lighthouse tower on the north end of Little Cumberland Island charted in approximate position latitude 30° 58.5'N. longitude 81° 24.8'W.

(c) A line drawn across the seaward extremity of the St. Marys Entrance Jetties.

§80.723 Amelia Island, FL to Cape Canaveral, FL.

(a) A line drawn from the southernmost extremity of Amelia Island to the northeasternmost extremity of Little Talbot Island.

(b) A line formed by the centerline of the highway bridge from Little Talbot Island to Fort George Island.

(c) A line drawn across the seaward extremity of the St. Johns River Entrance Jetties.

(d) A line drawn across the seaward extremity of the St. Augustine Inlet Jetties.

(e) A line formed by the centerline of the highway bridge over Matanzas Inlet.

(f) A line drawn across the seaward extremity of the Ponce de Leon Inlet Jetties.

§80.727 Cape Canaveral, FL to Miami Beach, FL.

(a) A line drawn across the seaward extremity of the Port Canaveral Entrance Channel Jetties.

(b) A line drawn across the seaward extremity of the Sebastian Inlet Jetties.

(c) A line drawn across the seaward extremity of the Fort Pierce Inlet Jetties.

(d) A north-south line (longitude 80° 09.7'W.) drawn across St. Lucie Inlet.

(e) A line drawn from the seaward extremity of Jupiter Inlet North Jetty to the northeast extremity of the concrete apron on the south side of Jupiter inlet.

(f) A line drawn across the seaward extremity of the Lake Worth Inlet Jetties.

(g) A line drawn across the seaward extremity of the Boynton Inlet Jetties.

(h) A line drawn from Boca Raton Inlet North Jetty Light 2 to Boca Raton Inlet South Jetty Light 1.

(i) A line drawn from Hillsboro Inlet Light to Hillsboro Inlet Entrance Light 2; thence to Hillsboro Inlet Entrance Light 1; thence west to the shoreline.

(j) A line drawn across the seaward extremity of the Port Everglades Entrance Jetties.

(k) A line formed by the centerline of the highway bridge over Bakers Haulover Inlet.

§80.730 Miami Harbor, FL.

A line drawn across the seaward extremity of the Miami Harbor Government Cut Jetties.

§80.735 Miami, FL to Long Key, FL.

(a) A line drawn from the southernmost extremity of Fisher Island 212° true to the point latitude 25° 45.0'N. longitude 80° 08.6'W. on Virginia Key.

(b) A line formed by the centerline of the highway bridge between Virginia Key and Key Biscayne.

(c) A line drawn from Cape Florida Light to the northern most extremity on Soldier Key.

(d) A line drawn from the southernmost extremity on Soldier Key to the northernmost extremity of the Ragged Keys.

(e) A line drawn from the Ragged Keys to the southernmost extremity of Angelfish Key following the general trend of the seaward shoreline.

(f) A line drawn on the centerline of the Overseas Highway (U.S. 1) and bridges from latitude 25° 19.3'N. longitude 80° 16.0'W. at Little Angelfish Creek to the radar dome charted on Long Key at approximate position latitude 24° 49.3'N. longitude 80° 49.2'W.

PUERTO RICO AND VIRGIN ISLANDS

SEVENTH DISTRICT

§80.738 Puerto Rico and Virgin Islands.

(a) Except inside lines specifically described in this section, the 72 COLREGS shall apply on all other bays, harbors and lagoons of Puerto Rico and the U.S. Virgin Islands.

(b) A line drawn from Puerto San Juan Light to Cabras Light across the entrance of San Juan Harbor.

GULF COAST

SEVENTH DISTRICT

§80.740 Long Key, FL to Cape Sable, FL.

A line drawn from the microwave tower charted on Long Key at approximate position latitude 24° 48.8'N. longitude 80° 49.6'W, to Long Key Light 1; thence to Arsenic Bank Light 2; thence to Sprigger Bank Light 5; thence to Schooner Bank Light 6; thence to Oxfoot Bank Light 10; thence to East Cape Light 2; thence through East Cape Daybeacon 1A to the shoreline at East Cape.

§80.745 Cape Sable, FL to Cape Romano, FL.

(a) A line drawn following the general trend of the mainland, highwater shoreline from Cape Sable at East Cape to Little Shark River Light 1; thence to westernmost extremity of Shark Point; thence following the general trend of the mainland, highwater shoreline crossing the entrances of Harney River, Broad Creek, Broad River, Rodgers River First Bay, Chatham River, Huston River, to the shoreline at coordinate latitude 25° 41.8'N. longitude 81° 17.9'W.

(b) The 72 COLREGS shall apply to the waters surrounding the Ten Thousand Islands and the bays, creeks, inlets, and rivers between Chatham Bend and Marco Island except inside lines specifically described in this part.

(c) A north-south line drawn at longitude 81° 20.2'W. across the entrance to Lopez River.

(d) A line drawn across the entrance to Turner River parallel to the general trend of the shoreline.

(e) A line formed by the centerline of Highway 92 Bridge at Goodland.

§80.748 Cape Romano, FL to Sanibel Island, FL.

(a) A line drawn across Big Marco Pass parallel to the general trend of the seaward, highwater shoreline.

(b) A line drawn from the northwesternmost extremity of Coconut Island 000°T across Capri Pass.

(c) Lines drawn across Hurricane and Little Marco Passes parallel to the general trend of the seaward, highwater shoreline.

(d) A line from the seaward extremity of Gordon Pass South Jetty 014° true to the shoreline at approximate coordinate latitude 26° 05.7'N. longitude 81° 48.1'W.

(e) A line drawn across the seaward extremity of Doctors Pass Jetties.

(f) Lines drawn across Wiggins, Big Hickory, New, and Big Cados Passes parallel to the general trend of the seaward highwater shoreland.

(g) A straight line drawn from Sanibel Island Light through Matanzas Pass Channel Light 2 to the shore of Estero Island.

§80.750 Sanibel Island, FL to St. Petersburg, FL.

(a) A line formed by the centerline of the highway bridge over Blind Pass, between Captiva Island and Sanibel Island, and lines drawn across Redfish and Captiva Passes parallel to the general trend of the seaward, highwater shorelines.

(b) A line drawn from La Costa Test Pile North Light to Port Boca Grande Light.

(c) Lines drawn across Gasparilla and Stump Pasees parallel to the general trend of the seaward, highwater shorelines.

(d) A line across the seaward extremity of Venice Inlet Jetties.

(e) A line drawn across Midnight Pass parallel to the general trend of the seaward, highwater shoreline.

(f) A line drawn from Big Sarasota Pass Light 14 to the southernmost extremity of Lido Key.

(g) A line drawn across New Pass tangent to the seaward, highwater shoreline of Longboat Key.

(h) A line drawn across Longboat Pass parallel to the seaward, highwater shoreline.

(i) A line drawn from the northwesternmost extremity of Bean Point to the southeasternmost extremity of Egmont Key.

(j) A straight line drawn from Egmont Key Light through Egmont Channel Range Rear Light to the shoreline on Mullet Key.

(k) A line drawn from the northernmost extremity of Mullet Key across Bunces Pass and South Channel to Pass-a-grille Channel Light 8; thence to Pass-a-grille Channel Daybeacon 9; thence to the southwesternmost extremity of Long Key.

§80.753 St. Petersburg, FL to Anclote, FL.

(a) A line drawn across Blind Pass, between Treasure Island and Long Key, parallel with the general trend of the seaward, highwater shoreline.

(b) Lines formed by the centerline of the highway bridges over Johns and Clearwater Passes.

(c) A line drawn across Dunedin and Hurricane Passes parallel with the general trend of the seaward, highwater shoreline.

(d) A line drawn from the northernmost extremity of Honeymoon Island to Anclote Anchorage South Entrance Light 7; thence to Anclote Key 28° 10.0'N, 82° 50.6'W; thence a straight line through Anclote River Cut B Range Rear Light to the shoreline.

§80.755 Anclote, FL to the Suncoast Keys, FL.

(a) Except inside lines specifically described in this section, the 72 COLREGS shall apply on the bays, bayous, creeks, marinas, and rivers from Anclote to the Suncoast Keys.

(b) A north-south line drawn at longitude 82° 38.3'W. across the Chassahowitzka River Entrance.

§80.757 Suncoast Keys, FL to Horseshoe Point, FL.

(a) Except inside lines specifically described in this section, the 72 COLREGS shall apply on the bays, bayous, creeks, and marinas from the Suncoast Keys to Horseshoe Point.

(b) A line formed by the centerline of Highway 44 Bridge over the Salt River.

(c) A north-south line drawn through Crystal River Entrance Daybeacon 25 across the river entrance.

(d) A north-south line drawn through the Cross Florida Barge Canal Daybeacon 48 across the canal.

(e) A north-south line drawn through Withlacoochee River Daybeacon 40 across the river.

(f) A line drawn from the westernmost extremity of South Point north to the shoreline across the Waccasassa River Entrance.

(g) A line drawn from position latitude 29° 16.6'N. longitude 83° 06.7'W. 300° true to the shoreline of Hog Island.

(h) A north-south line drawn through Suwannee River Wadley Pass Channel Daybeacons 30 and 31 across the Suwannee River.

§80.760 Horseshoe Point, FL to Rock Islands, FL.

(a) Except inside lines specifically described provided in this section, the 72 COLREGS shall apply on the bays, bayous, creeks, marinas, and dyers from Horseshoe Point to the Rock Islands.

(b) A north-south line drawn through Steinhatchee River Light 21.

(c) A line drawn from Fenholloway River Approach Light FR east across the entrance to Fenholloway River.

EIGHTH DISTRICT

§80.805 Rock Island, FL to Cape San Bras, FL.

(a) A north-south line drawn from the Econfina River Light to the opposite shore.

(b) A line drawn from Gamble Point Light to the southernmost extremity of Cabell Point.

(c) A line drawn from St. Marks (Range Rear) Light to St. Marks Channel Light 11; thence to the southernmost extremity of Live Oak Point; thence in a straight line through Shell Point Light to the southernmost extremity of Ochlockonee Point; thence to Bald Point along longitude 84° 20.5'W.

(d) A line drawn from the south shore of Southwest Cape at longitude 84° 22.7'W. to Dog Island Reef East Light 1; thence to Turkey Point Light 2; thence to the easternmost extremity of Dog Island.

(e) A line drawn from the westernmost extremity of Dog Island to the easternmost extremity of St. George Island.

(f) A line drawn across the seaward extremity of the St. George Island Channel Jetties.

(g) A line drawn from the north westernmost extremity of Sand Island to West Pass Light 7.

(h) A line drawn from the westernmost extremity oh St. Vincent Island to the southeast, high-water shoreline of Indian Peninsula at longitude 85° 13.5' W.

§80.810 Cape San Bias, FL to Perdido Bay, FL.

(a) A line drawn from St. Joseph Bay Entrance Range A Rear Light through St. Joseph Bay Entrance Range B Front Light to St. Joseph Point.

(b) A line drawn across the mouth of Salt Creek as an extension of the general trend of the shoreline to continue across the inlet to St. Andrews sound in the middle of Crooked Island.

(c) A line drawn from the northernmost extremity of Crooked Island 000°T. to the mainland.

(d) A line drawn from the easternmost extremity of Shell Island 120° true to the shoreline across the east entrance to St. Andrews Bay.

(e) A line drawn between the seaward end of the St. Andrews Bay Entrance Jetties.

(f) A line drawn between the seaward end of the Choctawatchee Bay Entrance Jetties.

(g) A east-west line drawn from Fort McRee Leading Light across the Pensacola Bay Entrance along latitude 30° 19.5'N.

(h) A line drawn between the seaward end of the Perdido Pass Jetties.

§80.815 Mobile Bay, AL to the Chandeleur Islands, LA.

(a) A line drawn across the in lets to Little Lagoon as an extension of the general trend of the shoreline.

(b) A line drawn from Mobile Point Light to Dauphin Island Channel Light No. 1 to the eastern corner of Fort Gaines at Pelican Point.

(c) A line drawn from the westernmost extremity of Dauphin Island to the easternmost extremity of Petit Bois Island.

(d) A line drawn from Horn Island Pass Entrance Range Front Light on Petit Bois Island to the easternmost extremity of Horn Island.

(e) A east-west line (latitude 30° 14.7'N.) drawn between the westernmost extremity of Horn Island to the easternmost extremity of Ship Island.

(f) A curved line drawn following the general trend of the seaward, highwater shoreline of Ship Island.

(g) A line drawn from Ship Island Light; to Chandeleur Light; thence in a curved line following the general trend of the seaward, highwater shorelines of the Chandeleur Islands to the island at latitude 29° 44.1' N. longitude 88° 53.0'W; thence to latitude 29° 26.5'N. longitude 88° 55.6'W.

§80.825 Mississippi Passes, LA.

(a) A line drawn from latitude 29° 26.5'N., longitude 88° 55.6'W. to latitude 29° 10.6'N., longitude 88° 59.8'W.; thence to latitude 29° 03.5'N., longitude 89° 03.7' W.; thence to latitude 28° 58.8'N., longitude 89° 04.3'W.

(b) A line drawn from latitude 28° 58.8'N. longitude 89° 04.3'W.; to latitude 28° 57.3'N., longitude 89° 05.3'W.; thence to latitude 28° 56.95'N., longitude 89° 05.6' W.; thence to latitude 29° 00.4'N. longitude 89° 09.8'W.; thence following the general trend of the seaward highwater shoreline in a northwesterly direction to latitude 29° 03.4'N., longitude 89° 13.0' W.; thence west to latitude 29° 03.5'N., longitude 89° 15.5'W.; thence following the general trend of the seaward highwater shoreline in a southwesterly direction to latitude 28° 57.7'N., longitude 89° 22.3'W.

(c) A line drawn from latitude 28° 57.7'N., longitude 89° 22.3' W.; to latitude 28° 51.4' N., longitude 89° 24.5' W.; thence to latitude 28° 51.5'N., longitude 89° 27.1'W.; thence to latitude 28° 52.65' N., longitude 89° 27.1'W.; thence to the seaward extremity of the Southwest Pass West Jetty located at latitude 28° 54.5'N. longitude 89° 26.1'W.

(d) A line drawn from Mississippi River South Pass East Jetty Light 4 to Mississippi River South Pass West Jetty Light; thence following the general trend of the seaward highwater shoreline in a northwesterly direction to coordinate latitude 29° 03.4'N. longitude 89° 13.0'W.; thence west to coordinate latitude 29° 03.5'N., longitude 89° 15.5'W., thence following the general trend of the seaward, highwater shoreline in a southwesterly direction to Mississippi River Southwest Pass Entrance Light.

(e) A line drawn from Mississippi River Southwest Pass Entrance Light; thence to the seaward extremity of the Southwest Pass West Jetty located at coordinate latitude 28° 54.5'N. longitude 89° 26.1'W.

§80.830 Mississippi Passes, LA to Point Au Fer, LA.

(a) A line drawn from the seaward extremity of the Southwest Pass West Jetty located at coordinate latitude 28° 54.5'N. longitude 89° 26.1'W.; thence following the general trend of the seaward, highwater jetty and shoreline in a north, northeasterly direction to Old Tower latitude 28° 58.8'N. longitude 89° 23.3'W.; thence to West Bay Light; thence to coordinate latitude 29° 05.2'N. longitude 89° 24.3'W.; thence a curved line following the general trend of the high-water shoreline to Point Au Fer Island except as otherwise described in this section.

(b) A line drawn across the seaward extremity of the Empire Waterway (Bayou Fontanelle) entrance jetties.

(c) An east-west line drawn from the westernmost extremity of Grand Terre Islands in the direction of 194° true to the Grand Isle Fishing Jetty Light.

(d) A line drawn between the seaward extremity of the Belle Pass Jetties.

(e) A line drawn from the westernmost extremity of the Tumbler Island to the easternmost extremity of Isles Dernieres.

(f) A north-south line drawn from Caillou Bay Light 13 across Caillou Boca.

(g) A line drawn 107° true from Caillou Bay Boat Landing Light across the entrances to Grand Bayou du Large and Bayou Grand Caillou.

(h) A line drawn on an axis of 103° true through Taylors Bayou Entrance Light 2 across the entrances to Jack Stout Bayou, Taylors Bayou, Pelican Pass, and Bayou de West.

§80.835 Point Au Fer, LA to Calcasieu Pass, LA.

(a) A line drawn from Point Au Fer to Atchafalaya Channel Light 34; thence Point Au Fer Reef Light 33; Atchafalaya Bay Pipeline Light D latitude 29° 25.0'N. longitude 91° 31.7'W.; thence Atchafalaya Bay Light 1 latitude 29° 25.3'N. longitude 91° 35.8'W.; thence South Point.

(b) Lines following the general trend of the highwater shoreline drawn across the bayou canal inlets from the Gulf of Mexico between South Point and Calcasieu Pass except as otherwise described in this section.

(c) A line drawn on an axis of 140° true through Southwest Pass-Vermillion Bay Light 4 across Southwest Pass.

(d) A line drawn across the seaward extremity of the Freshwater Bayou Canal Entrance Jetties.

(e) A line drawn from Mermentau Channel East Jetty Light 6 to Mermentau Channel West Jetty Light 7.

(f) A line drawn from the radio tower charted in approximate position latitude 29° 45.7'N. longitude 93° 06.3'W. 115° true across Mermentau Pass.

(g) A line drawn across the seaward extremity of the Calcasieu Pass Jetties.

§80.840 Sabine Pass, TX to Galveston, TX.

(a) A line drawn from the Sabine Pass East Jetty Light to the seaward end of the Sabine Pass West Jetty.

(b) A line drawn across the small boat passes through the Sabine Pass East and West Jetties.

(c) A line formed by the centerline of the highway bridge over Rollover Pass at Gilchrist.

§80.845 Galveston, TX to Freeport, TX.

(a) A line drawn from Galveston North Jetty Light 6A to Galveston South Jetty Light 5A.

(b) A line formed by the centerline of the highway bridge over San Luis Pass.

(c) Lines formed by the centerlines of the highway .bridges over the inlets to Christmas Bay (Cedar Cut) and Drum Bay.

(d) A line drawn from the seaward extremity of the Freeport North Jetty to Freeport Entrance Light 6; thence Freeport Entrance Light 7; thence the seaward extremity of Freeport South Jetty.

§80.850 Brazos River, TX to the Rio Grande, TX.

(a) Except as otherwise described in this section lines drawn continuing the general trend of the seaward, highwater shorelines across the inlets to Brazos River Diversion Channel, San Bernard River, Cedar Lakes, Brown Cedar Cut, Colorado River, Matagorda Bay, Cedar Bayou, Corpus Christi Bay, and Laguna Madre.

(b) A line drawn across the seaward extremity of Matagorda Ship Channel North Jetties.

(c) A line drawn from the seaward tangent of Matagorda Peninsula at Decros Point to Matagorda Light.

(d) A line drawn across the seaward extremity of the Aransas Pass Jetties.

(e) A line drawn across the seaward extremity of the Port Mansfield Entrance Jetties.

(f) A line drawn across the seaward extremity of the Brazos Santiago Pass Jetties.

PACIFIC COAST

ELEVENTH DISTRICT

§80.1105 Santa Catalina Island, CA.

The 72 COLREGS shall apply to the harbors on Santa Catalina Island.

§80.1110 San Diego Harbor, CA. A line drawn from Zuniga Jetty Light "V" to Zuniga Jetty Light "Z"; thence to Point Loma Light.

§80.111 5 Mission Bay, CA. A line drawn from Mission Bay South Jetty Light 2 to Mission Bay North Jetty Light 1.

§80.1120 Oceanside Harbor, CA. A line drawn from Oceanside South Jetty Light 4 to Oceanside Breakwater Light 3.

§80.1125 Dana Point Harbor, CA. A line drawn from Dana Point Jetty Light 6 to Dana Point Breakwater Light 5.

§80.1130 Newport Bay, CA. A line drawn from Newport Bay East Jetty Light 4 to Newport Bay West Jetty Light 3.

§80.1135 San Pedro Bay—Anaheim Bay, CA.

(a) A line drawn across the seaward extremities of the Anaheim Bay Entrance East Jetties; thence to Long Beach Breakwater East End Light 1.

(b) A line drawn from Long Beach Channel Entrance Light 2 to Long Beach Light.

(c) A line drawn from Los Angeles Main Entrance Channel Light 2 to Los Angeles Light.

§80.1140 Redondo Harbor, CA. A line drawn from Redondo Beach East Jetty Light 2 to Redondo Beach West Jetty Light 3.

§80.1145 Marina Del Rey, CA.

(a) A line drawn from Marina Del Rey Breakwater South Light 1 to Marina Del Rey Light 4.

(b) A line drawn from Marina Del Rey Breakwater North Light 2 to Marina Del Rey Light 3.

(c) A line drawn from Marina Del Rey Light 4 to the seaward extremity of the Ballona Creek South Jetty.

§80.1150 Port Husneme, CA. A line drawn from Port Hueneme East Jetty Light 4 to fort Hueneme West Jetty Light.

§80.1155 Channel Islands Harbor, CA.

(a) A line drawn from Channel Islands Harbor South Jetty Light 2 to Channel Islands Harbor Breakwater South Light 1.

(b) A line drawn from Channel Islands Harbor Breakwater North Light to Channel Islands Harbor North Jetty Light 5.

§80.1160 Ventura Marina, CA. A line drawn from Ventura Marina South Jetty Light 6 to Ventura Marina Breakwater South Light 3; thence to Ventura Marina North Jetty Light 7.

§80.1165 Santa Barbara Harbor, CA. A line drawn from Santa Barbara Harbor Light 4 to Santa Barbara Harbor Breakwater Light.

TWELFTH DISTRICT

§80.1205 San Luis Obispo Bay, CA. A line drawn from the southernmost extremity of Fossil Point to the seaward extremity of Whaler Island Breakwater.

§80.1210 Estero-Morro Bay, CA. A line drawn from the seaward extremity of the Morro Bay East Breakwater to the Morro Bay West Breakwater Light.

§80.1215 Monterey Harbor, CA. A line drawn from Monterey Harbor Light 6 to the northern extremity of Monterey Municipal Wharf 2.

§80.1220 Moss Landing Harbor, CA. A line drawn from the seaward extremity of the pier located 0.3 mile south of Moss Landing Harbor Entrance to the seaward extremity of the Moss Landing Harbor North Breakwater.

§80.1225 Santa Cruz Harbor, CA. A line drawn from the Seaward extremity of the Santa Cruz Harbor East Breakwater to Santa Cruz Harbor West Breakwater Light; thence to Santa Cruz Light.

§80.1230 Pillar Point Harbor, CA. A line drawn from Pillar Point Harbor Light 6 to Pillar Point Harbor Entrance Light.

§80.1250 San Francisco Harbor, CA. A straight line drawn from Point Bonita Light through Mile Rocks Light to the shore.

§80.1255 Bodega and Tomales Bay, CA.

(a) An east-west line drawn from Sand Point to Avails Beach.

(b) A line drawn from the seaward extremity of Bodega Harbor North Breakwater to Bodega Harbor Entrance Light 1.

§80.1260 Albion River, CA. A line drawn on an axis of 030° true through Albion River Light 1 across Albion Cove.

§80.1265 Noyo River, CA. A line drawn from Noyo River Entrance Daybeacon 4 to Noyo River Entrance Light 5.

§80.1270 Arcata-Humboldt Bay, CA. A line drawn from Humboldt Bay Entrance Light 4 to Humboldt Bay Entrance Light 3.

§80.1275 Crescent City Harbor, CA. A line drawn from Crescent City Entrance Light to the southeasternmost extremity of Whaler Island.

THIRTEENTH DISTRICT

§80.1305 Chetco River, OR. A line drawn across the seaward extremities of the Chetco River Entrance Jetties.

§80.1310 Rogue River, OR. A line drawn across the seaward extremities of the Rogue River Entrance Jetties.

§80.1315 Coquille River, OR. A line drawn across the seaward extremities of the Coquille River Entrance Jetties.

§80.1320 Coos Bay, OR. A line drawn across the seaward extremities of the Coos Bay Entrance Jetties.

§80.1325 Umpqua River, OR. A line drawn across the seaward extremities of the Umpqua Entrance Jetties.

§80.1330 Siuslaw River, OR. A line drawn across the seaward extremities of the Siuslaw River Entrance Jetties.

§80.1335 Alsea Bay, OR. A line drawn from the seaward shoreline on the north of the Alsea Bay Entrance 165° true across the channel entrance.

§80.1340 Yaquina Bay, OR. A line drawn across the seaward extremities of Yaquina Bay Entrance Jetties.

§80.1345 Depoe Bay, OR. A line drawn across the Depoe Bay Channel entrance parallel with the general trend of the highwater shoreline.

§80.1350 Netarts Bay, OR. A line drawn from the northernmost extremity of the shore on the south side of Netarts Bay north to the opposite shoreline.

§80.1355 Tillamook Bay, OR. A line drawn across the seaward extremities of the Tillamook Bay Entrance Jetties.

§80.1360 Nehalem River, OR. A line drawn approximately parallel with the general trend of the highwater shoreline across the Nehalem River Entrance.

§80.1365 Columbia River Entrance, OR/WA. A line drawn from the seaward extremity of the Columbia River North Jetty (above water) 155° true to the seaward extremity of the Columbia River South Jetty (above water).

§80.1370 Willapa Bay, WA. A line drawn from Willapa Bay Light 169.8° true to the westernmost tripod charted 1.6 miles south of Leadbetter Point.

§80.1375 Grays Harbor, WA. A line drawn across the sea ward extremities (above water) of the Grays Harbor Entrance Jetties.

§80.1380 Quillayute River, WA. A line drawn from the seaward extremity of the Quillayute River Entrance East Jetty to the overhead power cable tower charted on James Island; thence a straight line through Quillayute River Entrance Light 3 to the shoreline.

§80.1385 Strait of Juan de Fuca. The 72 COLREGS shall apply on all waters of the Strait of Juan de Fuca.

§80.1390 Haro Strait and Strait of Georgia. The 72 COLREGS shall apply on all waters of the Haro Strait and the Strait of Georgia.

§80.1395 Puget Sound and Adjacent Waters. The 72 COLREGS shall apply on all waters of Puget Sound and adjacent waters, including Lake Union, Lake Washington, Hood Canal, and all tributaries.

PACIFIC ISLANDS
FOURTEENTH DISTRICT

§80.1410 Hawaiian Island. Exemption from General Rule. Except as provided elsewhere in this part for Mamala Bay and Kaneohe Bay on Oahu; Port Allen and Nawiliwili Bay on Kauai; Kahului Harbor on Maui; and Kawailae and Hilo Harbors on Hawaii, the 72 COLREGS shall apply on all other bays, harbors, and lagoons of the Hawaiian Island (including Midway).

§80.1420 Mamala Bay, Oahu, HI. A line drawn from Barbers Point Light to Diamond Head Light.

§80.1430 Kaneohe Bay, Oahu, HI. A straight line drawn from Pyramid Rock Light across Kaneohe Bay through the center of Mokolii Island to the shoreline.

§80.1440 Port Allen, Kauai, HI. A line drawn from Hanapepe Light to Hanapepe Bay Breakwater Light.

§80.1450 Nawiliwili Harbor, Kauai, HI. A line drawn from Nawiliwili Harbor Breakwater Light to Kukii Point Light.

§80.1460 Kahului Harbor, Maui, HI. A line drawn from Kahului Harbor Entrance East Breakwater Light to Kahului Harbor Entrance West Breakwater Light.

§80.1470 Kawalhae Harbor, Hawaii, HI. A line drawn from Kawaihae Light to the seaward extremity of the Kawaihae South Breakwater.

§80.1480 Hilo Harbor, Hawaii, HI. A line drawn from the seaward extremity of the Hilo Breakwater 265° true (as an extension of the seaward side of the breakwater) to the shoreline 0.2 nautical mile north of Alealea Point.

§80.1490 Apra Harbor, U.S. Territory of Guam. A line drawn from the westernmost extremity of Orote Island to the westernmost extremity of Glass Breakwater.

§80.1495 U.S. Pacific Island Possessions. The 72 COLREGS shall apply on the bays, harbors, lagoons, and waters surrounding the U.S. Pacific Island Possessions of American Samoa, Baker, Canton, Howland, Jarvis, Johnson, Palmyra, Swains and Wake Island. (The Trust Territory of the Pacific Islands is not a U.S. possession, and therefore Part 82 does not apply thereto.)

ALASKA
SEVENTEENTH DISTRICT

§80.1705 Alaska. The 72 COLREGS shall apply on all the sounds, bays, harbors, and inlets of Alaska.

Penalty Provisions

VIOLATIONS OF INTERNATIONAL NAVIGATION RULES AND REGULATIONS (33 U.S.C. 1608)

(a) Whoever operates a vessel, subject to the provisions of this Act, in violation of this Act or of any regulation promulgated pursuant to section 8, shall be liable to a civil penalty of not more than $5,000 for each such violation.

(b) Every vessel subject to the provisions of this Act, other than a public vessel being used for noncommercial purposes, which is operated in violation of this Act or of any regulation promulgated pursuant to section 8, shall be liable to a civil penalty of not more than $5,000 for each such violation, for which penalty the vessel may be seized and proceeded against in the district court of the United States of any district within which such vessel may be found.

(c) The Secretary of the department in which the Coast Guard is operating may assess any civil penalty authorized by this section. No such penalty may be assessed until the person charged, or the owner of the vessel charged, as appropriate, shall have been given notice of the violation involved and an opportunity for a hearing. For good cause shown, the Secretary may remit, mitigate, or compromise any penalty assessed. Upon the failure of the person charged, or the owner of the vessel charged, to pay an assessed penalty, as it may have been mitigated or compromised, the Secretary may request the Attorney General to commence an action in the appropriate district court of the United States for collection of the penalty as assessed, without regard to the amount involved, together with such other relief as may be appropriate.

VIOLATIONS OF INLAND NAVIGATION RULES AND REGULATIONS (33 U.S.C. 2072)

(a) Whoever operates a vessel in violation of this Act, or of any regulation issued thereunder, or in violation of a certificate of alternative compliance issued under Rule 1 is liable to a civil penalty of not more than $5,000 for each violation.

(b) Every vessel subject to this Act, other than a public vessel being used for noncommercial purposes, that is operated in violation of this Act, or of any regulation issued thereunder, or in violation of a certificate of alternative compliance issued under Rule 1 is liable to a civil penalty of not more than $5,000 for each violation, for which penalty the vessel may be seized and proceeded against in the district court of the United States of any district within which the vessel may be found.

(c) The Secretary may assess any civil penalty authorized by this section. No such penalty may be assessed until the person charged, or the owner of the vessel charged, as appropriate, shall have been given notice of the violation involved and an opportunity for a hearing. For good cause shown, the Secretary may remit, mitigate, or compromise any penalty assessed. Upon the failure of the person charged, or the owner of the vessel charged, to pay an assessed penalty, as it may have been miti-

gated or compromised, the Secretary may request the Attorney General to commence an action in the appropriate district court of the United States for collection of the penalty as assessed, without regard to the amount involved, together with such other relief as may be appropriate.

(d) (1) If any owner, operator, or individual in charge of a vessel is liable for a penalty under this section, or if reasonable cause exists to believe that the owner, operator, or individual in charge may be subject to a penalty under this section, the Secretary of the Treasury, upon the request of the Secretary, shall with respect to such vessel refuse or revoke any clearance required by section 4197 of the Revised Statutes of the United States (46 App. U.S.C. 91).

(2) Clearance or a permit refused or revoked under this subsection may be granted upon filing of a bond or other surety satisfactory to the Secretary.

PENALTIES FOR NEGLIGENT OPERATIONS; DUTIES RELATED TO MARINE CASUALTY ASSISTANCE AND INFORMATION; DUTY TO PROVIDE ASSISTANCE AT SEA; INJUNCTIONS (46 U.S.C. 2301-2305) EXCERPT FROM TITLE 46 OF THE UNITED STATES CODE CHAPTER 23 OPERATIONS OF VESSELS GENERALLY

[Enacted on August 26, 1983]

2301 Application.

2302 Penalties for negligent operations.

2303 Duties related to marine casualty assistance.

2304 Duty to provide assistance at sea.

2305 Injunctions.

2306 Vessel Reporting Requirements.

§2301 Application.

This chapter applies to a vessel operated on waters subject to the jurisdiction of the United States and, for a vessel owned in the United States, on the high seas.

§2302 Penalties for negligent operations.

(a) A person operating a vessel in a negligent manner that endangers the life, limb, or property of a person is liable to the United States Government for a civil penalty of not more than $1,000.

(b) A person operating a vessel in a grossly negligent manner that endangers the life, limb, or property of a person shall be fined not more than $5,000, imprisoned for not more than one year, or both.

(c) An individual who is under the influence of alcohol, or a dangerous drug in violation of a law of the United States when operating a vessel, as determined under standards prescribed by the Secretary by regulation—

(1) is liable to the United States Government for a civil penalty of not more than $1,000 for a first violation and not more than $5,000 for a subsequent violation; or

(2) commits a class A misdemeanor.

(d) For a penalty imposed under this section, the vessel also is liable in rem unless the vessel is—

(1) owned by a State or a political subdivision of a State;

(2) operated principally for governmental purposes; and

(3) identified clearly as a vessel of that State or subdivision.

§2303 Duties related to marine casualty assistance and information.

(a) The master or individual in charge of a vessel involved in a marine casualty shall—

(1) render necessary assistance to each individual affected to save that affected individual from danger caused by the marine casualty, so far as the master or individual in charge can do so without serious danger to the master's or individual's vessel or to individuals on board; and

(2) give the master's or individual's name and address and identification of the vessel to the master or individual in charge of any other vessel involved in the casualty, to any individual injured, and to the owner of any property damaged.

(b) An individual violating this section or a regulation prescribed under this section shall be fined not more than $1,000 or imprisoned for not more than 2 years. The vessel also is liable in rm to the United States Government for the fine.

(c) An individual complying with subsection (a) of this section or gratuitously and in good faith rendering assistance at the scene of a marine casualty without objection by an individual assisted, is not liable for damages as a result of rendering assistance or for an act or omission in providing or arranging salvage, towage, medical treatment, or other assistance when the individual acts as an ordinary, reasonable, and prudent individual would have acted under the circumstances.

§2304 Duty to provide assistance at sea.

(a) A master or individual in charge of a vessel shall render assistance to any individual found at sea in danger of being lost, so far as the master or individual in charge can do so without serious danger to the master's or individual's vessel or individuals on board.

(b) A master or individual violating this section shall be fined not more than $1,000, imprisoned for not more than 2 years, or both.

§2305 Injunctions.

(a) The district courts of the United States have jurisdiction to enjoin the negligent operation of vessels prohibited by this chapter on the petition of the Attorney General for the United States Government.

(b) When practicable, the Secretary shall—

(1) give notice to any person against whom an action for injunctive relief is considered under this section an opportunity to present that person's views; and

(2) except for a knowing and willful violation, give the person a reasonable opportunity to achieve compliance.

(c) The failure to give notice and opportunity to present views under subsection (b) of this section does not preclude the court from granting appropriate relief.

§2306 Vessel Reporting Requirements

(a)(1) An owner, charterer, managing operator, or agent of a vessel of the United States, having reason to believe (because of lack of communication with or nonappearance of a vessel or any other incident) that the vessel may have been lost or imperiled, immediately shall—

(A) notify the Coast Guard; and

(B) use all available means to determine the status of the vessel.

(2) When more than 48 hours have passed since the owner, charterer, managing operator, or agent of a vessel required to report to the United States Flag Merchant Vessel Location Filing 203 System under authority of section 212 (A) of the Merchant Marine Act, 1936 (46 App. U.S. C. 1122a), has received a communication from the vessel, the owner, charterer, managing operator, or agent immediately shall—

(A) notify the Coast Guard; and

(B) use all available means to determine the status of the vessel.

(3) A person notifying the Coast Guard under paragraph (1) or (2) of this subsection shall providethe name and identification number of the vessel, the names of individuals on board, and other information that may be requested by the Coast Guard. The owner, charterer, managing operator, or agent also shall submit written confirmation to the Coast Guard 24 hours after nonwritten notification to the Coast Guard under those paragraphs.

(4) An owner, charterer, managing operator, or agent violating this subsection is liable to the United States Government for a civil penalty of not more than $5,000 for each day during which the violation occurs.

(b)(1) The master of a vessel of the United States required to report to the System shall report to the owner, charterer, managing operator, or agent at least once every 48 hours.

(2) A master violating this subsection is liable to the Government for a civil penalty of not more than $1,000 for each day during which the violation occurs.

(c) The Secretary may prescribe regulations to carry out this section.

Alternative Compliance

The alternative compliance procedures for the International Rules and the Inland Rules are the same, although they appear both in the International Rules section of the Code of Federal Regulations (33 CFR Part 81) and in the Inland Rules section (33 CFR Part 89).

1. Definitions.
2. General.
3. Application for a certificate of alternative compliance.
4. Certificate of alternative compliance: Contents.
5. Certificate of alternative compliance: Termination.
6. Record of certificaton of vessels of special construction or purpose.

1. Definitions.

As used in this part:

"72 COLREGS" refers to the International Regulations for Preventing Collisions at Sea, 1972, done at London, October 20, 1972, as rectified by the Proces-Verbal of December 1, 1973, as amended.

"Inland Rules" refers to the Inland Navigation Rules contained in the Inland Navigational Rules Act of 1980 (Pub. L. 96-591) and the technical annexes established under that act.

"A vessel of special construction or purpose" means a vessel designed or modified to perform a special function and whose arrangement is thereby made relatively inflexible.

"Interference with the special function of the vessel" occurs when installation or use of lights, shapes, or sound-signaling appliances under the 72 COLREGS/Inland Rules prevents or significantly hinders the operation in which the vessel is usually engaged.

2. General.

Vessels of special construction or purpose which cannot fully comply with the light, shape, and sound signal provisions of the 72 COLREGS/Inland Rules without interfering with their special function may instead meet alternative requirements. The Chief of the Marine Safety Division in each Coast Guard District Office makes this determination and requires that alternative compliance be as close as possible with the 72 COLREGS/Inland Rules. These regulations set out the procedure by which a vessel may be certified for alternative compliance.

3. Application for a Certificate of Alternative Compliance.

(a) The owner, builder, operator, or agent of a vessel of special construction or purpose who believes the vessel cannot fully comply with the 72 COLREGS/Inland Rules light, shape, or sound signal provisions without interference with its special function may apply for a determination that alternative compliance is justified. The application must be in writing, submitted to the Chief of the Marine Safety Division of the Coast Guard District in which the vessel is being built or operated, and include the following information:

(1) The name, address, and telephone number of the applicant.

(2) The identification of the vessel by its—

(i) Official number;

(ii) Shipyard hull number;

(iii) Hull identification number; or

(iv) State number, if the vessel does not have an official number or hull identification number.

(3) Vessel name and home port, if known.

(4) A description of the vessel's area of operation.

(5) A description of the provision for which the Certificate of Alternative Compliance is sought, including:

(i) The 72 COLREGS/Inland Rules Rule or Annex section number for which the Certificate of Alternative Compliance is sought;

(ii) A description of the special function of the vessel that would be interfered with by full compliance with the provision of that Rule or Annex section; and

(iii) A statement of how full compliance would interfere with the special function of the vessel.

(6) A description of the alternative installation that is in closest possible compliance with the applicable 72 COLREGS/Inland Rules Rule or Annex section.

(7) A copy of the vessel's plans or an accurate scale drawing that clearly shows—

(i) The required installation of the equipment under the 72 COLREGS/Inland Rules,

(ii) The proposed installation of the equipment for which certification as being sought, and

(iii) Any obstructions that may interfere with the equipment when installed in—

(A) The required location; and

(B) The proposed location.

(b) The Coast Guard may request from the applicant additional information concerning the application.

4. Certificate of Alternative Compliance: Contents.

The Chief of the Marine Safety Division issues the Certificate of Alternative Compliance to the vessel based on a determination that it cannot comply fully with 72 COLREGS/Inland Rules light, shape, and sound signal provisions without interference with its special function.

This Certificate includes—

(a) Identification of the vessel as supplied in the application;

(b) The provision of the 72 COLREGS/Inland Rules for which the Certificate authorizes alternative compliance;

(c) A certification that the vessel is unable to comply fully with the 72 COLREGS/Inland Rules light, shape, and sound signal requirements without interference with its special function;

(d) A statement of why full compliance would interfere with the special function of the vessel;

(e) The required alternative installation;

(f) A statement that the required alternative installation is in the closest possible compliance with the 72 COLREGS/Inland Rules without interfering with the special function of the vessel;

(g) The date of issuance;

(h) A statement that the Certificate of Alternative Compliance terminates when the vessel ceases to be usually engaged in the operation for which the certificate is issued.

5. Certificate of Alternative Compliance: Termination.

The Certificate of Alternative Compliance terminates if the information supplied under 3(a) or the Certificate issued under 4 is no longer applicable to the vessel.

6. Record of certification of vessels of special construction or purpose.

(a) Copies of Certificates of Alternative Compliance and documentation concerning Coast Guard vessels are available for inspection at Coast Guard Headquarters, Office of Navigation Safety and Waterway Services, 2100 Second Street, S.W., Washington, D.C. 20593.

(b) The owner or operator of a vessel issued a Certificate shall ensure that the vessel does not operate unless the Certificate of Alternative Compliance or a certified copy of that Certificate is on board the vessel and available for inspection by Coast Guard personnel.

Waters Specified By the Secretary

33 CFR Waters upon which Inland Rules 9(a)(ii), 14(d), 15(b) apply.

Inland Rules 9(a)(ii), 14(d), and 15(b) apply on the Great Lakes, the Western Rivers, and the following specified waters:

(a) Tennessee Tombigbee Waterway;

(b) Tombigbee River;

(c) Back Warrior River;

(d) Alabama River;

(e) Coosa River;

(f) Mobile River above the Cochrane Bridge at St. Louis Point;

(g) Flint River;

(h) Chattahoochee River; and

(i) The Apalachicola River above its confluence with the Jackson River.

33 CFR §89.27 Waters upon which Inland Rule 24(i) applies.

(a) Inland Rule 24(i) applies on the Western Rivers and the specified waters listed in §89.25 (a) through (i).

(b) Inland Rule 24(i) applies on the Gulf Intracoastal Waterway from St. Marks, Florida, to the Rio Grande, Texas, including the Morgan City-Pod Allen Alternate Route and the Galveston Freeport Cutoff, except that a power-driven vessel pushing ahead or towing alongside shall exhibit the lights required by Inland Rule 24(c), while transiting within the following areas:

(1) St Andrews Bay from the Hathaway Fixed Bridge at Mile 284.6 East of Harvey Locks (EHL) to the DuPont Fixed Bridge at Mile 295.4 EHL

(2) Pensacola Bay Santa Rosa Sound and Big Lagoon from the Light "10" off of Trout Point at Mile 176.9 EHL to the Pensacola Fixed Bridge at Mile 189.1 EHL

(3) Mobile Bay and Bon Secour Bay from the Dauphin Island Causeway Fixed Bridge at Mile 127.7 EHL to Little Point Clear at Mile 140 EHL

(4) Mississippi Sound from Grand Island Waterway Light "1" at Mile 53.8 EHL to Light "40" off the West Point of Dauphin Island at Mile 118.7 EHL

(5) The Mississippi River at New Orleans Mississippi River-Gulf Outlet Canal and the Inner Hareor Navigation Canal from the junction of the Harvey Canal and the Algiers Altemate Route at Mile 6.5 West of Harvey Locks (WHL) to the Michoud Canal at Mile 18 EHL

(6) The Calcasieu River from the Calcasieu Lock at Mile 238.6 WHL to the Emender Ufl Bridge at Mile 243.6 WHL

(7) The Sabine Neches Canal from Mile 262.5 WHL to Mile 291.5 WHL

(8) Bolivar Roads from the Bolivar Assembling Basin at Mile 346 WHL to the Galveston Causeway Bridge at Mile 357.3 WHL

(9) Freeport Harbor from Surfside Beach Fixed Bridge at Mile 393.8 WHL to the Bryan Beach Pontoon Bridge at Mile 397.6 WHL

(10) Matagorda Ship Channel area of Matagorda Bay from Range SKY Front Light at Mile 468.7 WHL to the Port O Connor Jetty at Mile 472.2 WHL

(11) Corpus Christi Bay from Reddish Bay Day Beacon "55" at Mile 537.4 WHL when in the Gulf Intracoastal Waterway main route or from the north end of Lydia Ann Island Mile 531.1A when in the Gulf Intracoastal Waterway Alternate Route to Corpus Christi Bay LT 76 at Mile 543.7 WHL

(12) Port Isabel and Brownsville Ship Channel south of the Padre Island Causeway Fixed Bridge Mile 665.1 WHL

Vessel Bridge-to-Bridge Radiotelephone Regulations

The Vessel Bridge-to-Bridge Radiotelephone Act is applicable on navigable waters of the United States inside the boundary lines established in 46 CFR 7. In all cases, the Act applies on waters subject to the Inland Rules. In some instances, the Act may apply all the way out to the three mile limit, depending on where the boundary lines are located. In no instance does the Act apply beyond the three mile limit.

26.01 Purpose.

26.02 Definitions.

26.03 Radiotelephone required.

26.04 Use of the designated frequency.

26.05 Use of radiotelephone.

26.06 Maintenance of radiotelephone.

26.07 Communications.

26.08 Exemption procedures.

26.09 List of exemptions.

§ 26.01 Purpose.

(a) The purpose of this part is to implement the provisions of the Vessel Bridge-to-Bridge Radiotelephone Act. This part—

(1) Requires the use of the vessel bridge-to-bridge radiotelephone;

(2) Provides the Coast Guard's interpretation of the meaning of important terms in the Act;

(3) Prescribes the procedures for applying for an exemption from the Act and the regulations issued under the Act and a listing of exemptions.

(b) Nothing in this part relieves any person from the obligation of complying with the rules of the road and the applicable pilot rules.

§ 26.02 Definitions.

For the purpose of this part and interpreting the Act—

"Secretary" means the Secretary of the Department in which the Coast Guard is operating;

"Act" means the " Vessel Bridge-to-Bridge Radiotelephone Act" 33 U.S.C. sections 1201-1208;

"Length" is measured from end to end over the deck excluding sheer, "Power-driven vessel" means any vessel propelled by machinery;

"Towing vessel" means any commercial vessel engaged in towing another vessel astern, alongside, or by pushing ahead;

"Vessel Traffic Services (VTS)" means a service implemented under Part 161 of this chapter by the United States Coast Guard designed to improve the safety and efficiency of vessel traffic and to protect the environment. The VTS has the capability to interact with marine traffic and respond to traffic situations developing in the VTS area; and

"Vessel Traffic Service Area or VTS Area" means the geographical area encompassing a specific VTS area of service as described in Part 161 of this chapter. This area of service may be subdivided into sectors for the purpose of allocating responsibility to individual Vessel Traffic Centers or to identify different operating requirements.

Note: Although regulatory jurisdiction is limited to the navigable waters of the United States, certain vessels will be encouraged or may be required, as a condition of port entry, to report beyond this area to facilitate traffic management within the VTS area.

§ 26.03 Radiotelephone required.

(a) Unless an exemption is granted under §26.09 and except as provided in paragraph (a) (4) of this section, this part applies to:

    (1) Every power-driven vessel of ≥20 m in length while navigating;

    (2) Every vessel of 100 gross tons and upward carrying one or more passengers for hire while navigating;

    (3) Every towing vessel of 26 feet or over in length while navigating.

    (4) Every dredge and floating plant engaged in or near a channel or fairway in operations likely to restrict or affect navigation of other vessels except for an unmanned or intermittently manned floating plant under the control of a dredge,

(b) Every vessel, dredge, or floating plant described in paragraph (a) of this section must have a radiotelephone on board capable of operation from its navigational bridge, or in the case of a dredge, from its main control station, and capable of transmitting and receiving on the frequency or frequencies within the 156-162 Megahertz band using the classes of emissions designated by the Federal Communications Commission for the exchange of navigational information.

(c) The radiotelephone required by paragraph (b) of this section must be carried on board the described vessels, dredges, and floating plants upon the navigable waters of the United States.

(d) The radiotelephone required by paragraph (b) of this section must be capable of transmitting and receiving on VHF FM channel 22A (157.1 MHz).

(e) While transiting any of the following waters, each vessel described in paragraph (a) of this section also must have on board a radiotelephone capable of transmitting and receiving on VHF FM channel 67 (156.375 MHz):

> (1) The lower Mississippi River from the territorial sea boundary, and within either the Southwest Pass safety fairway or the South Pass safety fairway specified in 33 CFR 166.200, to mile 242.4 AHP (Above Head of Passes) near Baton Rouge;

> (2) The Mississippi River-Gulf Outlet from the territorial sea boundary, and within the Mississippi River-Gulf Outlet Safety Fairway specified in 33 CFR 166.200, to that channel's junction with the Inner Harbor Navigation Canal; and

> (3) The full length of the Inner Harbor Navigation Canal from its junction with the Mississippi River to that canal's entry to Lake Pontchartrain at the New Seabrook vehicular bridge.

(f) In addition to the radiotelephone required by paragraph (b) of this section, each vessel described in paragraph (a) of this section while transiting any waters within a Vessel Traffic Service Area, must have on board a radiotelephone capable of transmitting and receiving on the VTS designated frequency in Table 26.03 (VTS Call Signs, Designated Frequencies, and Monitoring Areas).

Note: A single VHF-FM radio capable of scanning or sequential monitoring (often referred to as "dual watch" capability) will not meet the requirements for two radios.

§ 26.04 Use of the designated frequency.

(a) No person may use the frequency designated by the Federal Communications Commission under sections of the Act, 33 U.S.C. 1207(a), to transmit any information other than information necessary for the safe navigation of vessels or necessary tests.

(b) Each person who is required to maintain a listening watch under section 5 of the Act shall, when necessary, transmit and confirm, on the designated frequency, the intentions of his vessel and any other information necessary for the safe navigation of vessels.

(c) Nothing in these regulations may be construed as prohibiting the use of the designated frequency to communicate with shore stations to obtain or furnish information necessary for the safe navigation of vessels.

(d) On the navigable waters of the United States, Channel 13 (156.65 MHz) is the designated frequency required to be monitored in accordance with §26.05(a) except that in the area prescribed in §26.03(e), Channel 67 (156.375 MHz) is an additional frequency.

(e) On those navigable waters of the United States within a VTS area, the designated VTS frequency is the designated frequency required to be monitored in accordance with §26.05.

Note: As stated in 47 CFR 80.148(b), a VHF watch on Channel 16 (156.800Mhz) is not required on vessels subject to the Vessel Bridge-to-Bridge Radiotelephone Act and participating in a Vessel Traffic Service (VTS) system when the watch is maintained on both the vessel bridge-to-bridge frequency and a designated VTS frequency.

§ 26. 05 Use of Radiotelephone.

Section 5 of the Act states that:

The radiotelephone required by this Act is for the exclusive use of the master or person in charge of the vessel, or the person designated by the master or person in charge to pilot or direct the movement of the vessel, who shall maintain a listening watch on the designated frequency. Nothing contained herein shall be interpreted as precluding the use of portable radiotelephone equipment to satisfy the requirements of this Act.

§ 26.06 Maintenance of radiotelephone; failure of radiotelephone.

Section 6 of the Act states that:

Whenever radiotelephone capability is required by this Act, a vessel's radiotelephone equipment shall be maintained in effective operating condition. If the radiotelephone equipment carried aboard a vessel ceases to operate, the master shall exercise due diligence to restore it or cause it to be restored to effective operating condition at the earliest practicable time. The failure of a vessel's radiotelephone equipment shall not, in itself, constitute a violation of this Act, nor shall it obligate the master of any vessel to moor or anchor his vessel; however, the loss of radiotelephone capability shall be given consideration in the navigation of the vessel.

§ 26.07 Communications.

No person may use the services of, and no person may serve as, a person required to maintain a listening watch under section 5 of the Act, 33 U.S.C. 1204, unless the person can communicate in the English language.

§ 26.08 Exemption procedures.

(a) The Commandant has redelegated to the Assistant Commandant for Marine Safety and Environmental Protection, U.S. Coast Guard Headquarters, with the reservation that this authority shall not be further redelegated, the authority to grant exemptions from provisions of the Vessel Bridge-to-Bridge Radiotelephone Act and this part.

(b) Any person may petition for an exemption from any provision of the Act or this part;

(c) Each petition must be submitted in writing to U.S. Coast Guard (G-NSR), 2100 Second Street, SW, Washington, D.C. 20593-0001, and must state:

(1) The provisions of the Act or this part from which an exemption is requested; and

(2) The reasons why marine navigation will not be adversely affected if the exemption is granted and if the exemption relates to a local communication system how that system would fully comply with the intent of the concept of the Act but would not conform in detail if the exemption is granted.

§ 26.09 List of Exemptions.

(a) All vessels navigating on those waters governed by the navigation rules for the Great Lakes and their connecting and tributary waters (33 U.S.C. 241 et seq.) are exempt from the requirements of the Vessel Bridge-to-Bridge Radiotelephone Act and this part until May 6, 1975.

(b) Each vessel navigating on the Great Lakes as defined in the Inland Navigation Rules Act of 1980 (33 U.S.C. 2001 et seq.) and to which the Vessel Bridge-to-Bridge Radiotelephone Act (33 U.S.C. 1201-1208) applies is exempt from the requirements in 33 U.S.C. 1203, 1204, and 1205 and the regulations under §§26.03, 26.04, 26.05, 26.06, and 26.07. Each of these vessels and each person to whom 33 U.S.C. 1208(a) applies must comply with Articles VII, X, XI, XII, XIII, XV, and XVI and Technical Regulations 1-9 of "The Agreement Between the United States of America and Canada for Promotion of Safety on the Great Lakes by Means of Radio, 1973."

TABLE 26.03 - VESSEL TRAFFIC SERVICES (VTS) CALL SIGNS, DESIGNATED FREQUENCIES, AND MONITORING AREAS

VTS[1] (Call Sign)	DESIGNATED FREQUENCY (CH)[2]	MONITORING AREA
NEW YORK[3] New York Traffic [3]	156.700 MHZ (Ch.14) 156.550 MHZ (Ch.11)	The waters of the Lower New York Bay west of a line drawn from Norton Point to Breezy Point and north of a line drawn from Ambrose Entrance Lighted Gong Buoy #1 to Ambrose channel Lighted Gong Buoy #9 thence to West Bank Light and thence to Great Kills Light. The waters of the Upper New York Bay, south of 40° 42.40'N. (Brooklyn Bridge) and 40° 43.70'N. (Holland Tunnel Ventilator Shaft); and in Newark Bay, north of 40°38.25'N. (Arthur Kill Railroad Bridge), and south of 40° 41.95'N. (Lehigh Draw Bridge); and the Kill Van Kull.
		The waters of Raritan Bay east of a line drawn from Great Kills Light to Point Comfort in New Jersey and south of a line drawn from Great Kills Light to West Bank Light thence to Ambrose Channel Lighted Gong Buoy #9, and thence to Ambrose Channel Lighted Gong Buoy #1 and west of a line drawn from Ambrose Channel Lighted Gong Buoy #1 to the Sandy Hook Channel Entrance Buoys (Lighted Gong Buoys #1 and #2).
	156.600 MHZ (Ch.12)	Each vessel at anchor within the above areas.
HOUSTON [3] Houston Traffic	156.550 MHZ(Ch.11) 156.600 MHZ (Ch.12)	The navigable waters north of 29° N., west of 94° 20'W., south of 29° 49'N., and east of 95° 20'W.
		The navigable waters north of a line extending due west from the southern most end of Exxon Dock #1 (29° 43.37'N, 95° 01.27'W.)
BERWICK BAY Berwick Traffic	156.550 MHz (Ch.11)	The navigational waters south of 29° 45'N, west of 91°10'W, north of 29° 37'N, and east of 91° 18'W.
ST. MARY'S RIVER Soo Control	156.600 MHz (Ch.12)	The navigable waters of the St. Marys River between 45° 57'N. (De Tour Reef Light) and 46° 38.7'N. (Ile Parisienne Light), except the St. Marys Falls Canal and those navigable waters east of a line from 46° 04.16'N. and 46° 01.57'N. (La Pointe to Sims Point in Patagannissing Bay and Worsley Bay).
SAN FRANCISCO [3] San Francisco Offshore Vessel Movement Reporting Service	156.600 MHZ (Ch.12)	The waters within a 38 nautical mile radius of Mount Tamalpais (37° 55.8'N,122° 34.6'W) excluding the San Francisco Offshore Precautionary Area.
San Francisco Traffic	156.700 MHZ (Ch.14)	The waters of the San Francisco Offshore Precautionary Area eastward to San Francisco Bay including its tributaries extending to the pops of Stockton, Sacramento and Redwood City.

PUGET SOUND[5]

Seattle Traffic[6]	156.700 MHz (Ch. 14)	The navigable waters of Puget Sound, Hood Canal and adjacent waters south of a line connecting Marrowstone Point and Lagoon Point in Admiralty inlet and south of a line drawn due east from the southernmost tip of Possession Point on Whidbey Island to the shoreline.
	156.250 MHz (Ch. 5A)	The navigable waters of the Strait of Juan de Fuca east of 124° 40'W. excluding the waters in the central portion of the Strait of Juan de Fuca north and east of Race Rocks; the navigable waters of the Strait of Georgia east of 122° 52'W.; the San Juan Island Archipelago, Rosario Strait, Bellingham Bay; Admiralty Inlet north of a line connecting Marrowstone Point and Lagoon Point and all waters east of Whidbey Island north of a line drawn due east from the southernmost tip of Possession Point on Whidbey Island to the shoreline.
Tofino Traffic[7]	156.725 MHz (Ch. 74)	The waters west of 124° 40'W. within 50 nautical miles of the coast of Vancouver Island including the waters north of 48° N., and east of 127° W. Vancouver Traffic
Vancouver Traffic	156.550 MHz (Ch. 11)	The navigable waters of the Strait of Georgia west of 122° 52'W., the navigable waters of the central Strait of Juan de Fuca north and east of Race Rocks, Including the Gulf Island Archipelago, Boundary Pass and Haro Strait.

PRINCE WILLIAM SOUND[8]

Valdez Traffic	156.650 MHz (Ch. 13)	The navigable waters south of 61° 05'N., east of 147° 20'W., north of 60° N., and west of 146° 30' W.; and, all navigable waters in Port Valdez.

LOUISVILLE[8]

Louisville Traffic	156.650 MHz (Ch. 13)	The navigable waters of the Ohio River between McAlpine Locks (Mile 606) and Twelve Mile Island (Mile 593), only when the McAlpine upper pool gauge is at approximately 13.0 feet or above.

NOTES: 1. VTS regulations are denoted in 33 DFR Plan 161.A1 geography coordinates (latitude and longitude) are expressed in North American Datum of 1383 (NAD 83). 2. In the event of a communication failure either by the vessel traffic center or the vessel or radio congestion on a designated VTS frequency, communications may be established on an alternate VTS frequency. The bridge-to-bridge navigational frequency 145.650MHZ (Ch.13), is monitored in each VTS area; and it may be used as an alternate frequency, however, only to the extent that doing so provides a level of safety beyond that provided by other means. 3. Designated frequency monitoring is required within U.S. navigable waters. In areas which are outside the U.S. navigable waters, designated frequency monitoring is voluntary. However, prospective VTS Users are encouraged to monitor the designated frequency. 4. A Cooperative Vessel Traffic Service was established by the United States and Canada within adjoining waters. The appropriate vessel traffic center administers the rules issued by both nations; however, it will enforce only its own set of rules within its jurisdiction. 5. Seame Traffic may direct a vessel to monitor the other primary VTS frequency 156.250MHZ or 145.700MHZ (Ch.5a or 14) depending on traffic density, weather conditions or other safety factors, rather than strictly adhere to its to the designated frequency required for each monitoring area as defined above. This does not require a vessel t o monitor both primary frequencies. 6. A portion of Tofino Sectors monitoring area extends beyond the defined CVTS area. Designated frequency monitoring is voluntary in these portions outside the VTS jurisdiction, however, prospective VTS users are encouraged to monitor the designated frequency. 7. The bridge-to-bridge navigational frequency, 145.650MHZ (Ch.13), is used in these VTSs because the level of radiotelephone transmissions does not warrant a designated VTS frequency. The listening watch required by 526. 05 of this chapter is not limited to the monitoring area. 8. The bridge-to-bridge navigational frequency 156.650 MHz (Channel 13) is used in these VTSs because the level of radiotelephone transmissions does not warrant a designated VTS frequency. The listening watch required by 26.05 of this chapter is not limited to the monitoring area.

Legal Citations

72 COLREGS

International Navigational Rules Public Law 95-75
Act of 1977 . . . . 91 Stat.308; 33 U.S.C. 1601-1608
COLREGS Demarcation Lines . . . . 33 CFR 80
72 COLREGS: Implementing Rules . . . . 33 CFR 81
72 COLREGS: Interpretative Rules . . . . 33 CFR 82
Amendments to 72 COLREGS effective June 1, 1983 . . . . 48 FR 28634

INLAND RULES

Inland Navigational Rules Act of 1980 . . . . Public Law 96-591;
94 Stat. 3415;
33 U.S.C. 2001-2038
Annex I: Positioning and Technical Details of Lights and Shapes . . . . 33 CFR 84
Annex II: Additional Signals for Fishing in Close Proximity . . . . 33 CFR 85
Annex III: Technical Details of Sound Signal Appliances . . . . 33 CFR 86
Annex IV: Distress Signals . . . . 33 CFR 87
Annex V: Pilot Rules . . . . 33 CFR 88
Inland Navigation Rules: Implementing Rules . . . . 33 CFR 89
Inland Navigation Rules: Interpretative Rules . . . . 33 CFR 90

VESSEL BRIDGE-TO-BRIDGE RADIOTELEPHONE

Vessel Bridge-to-Bridge Radiotelephone Act . . . . Public Law 92-63;
85 Stat. 164;
33 U.S.C. 1201-1208
Vessel Bridge-to-Bridge Radiotelephone 33 CFR 26
Regulations (Coast Guard regulations)
Radiotelephone Stations Provided for
Compliance With the Vessel Bridge-to Bridge
Radiotelephone Act (Federal Communications
Commission regulations)
Other FCC regulations pertaining to vessel
bridge-to-bridge radiotelephone communications
are contained in various sections of 47 CFR 80.1001-80.1023
Boundary Lines . . . . 46 CFR 7

Conversion Table

Metric	U.S. Customary/Imperial Units
1000 M	3280.8 ft.
500 M	1640.4 ft.
200 M	656.2 ft.
150 M	492.1 ft.
100 M	328.1 ft.
75 M	246.1 ft.
60 M	196.8 ft.
50 M	164.0 ft.
25 M	82.0 ft.
20 M	65.6 ft.
12M	39.4 ft.
10M	32.8 ft.
8M	26.2 ft.
7M	23.0 ft.
6M	19.7 ft.
5 M	16.4 ft.
4.5M	14.8 ft.
4.0 M	13.1 ft.
3.5 M	11.5 ft.
2.5 M	8.2 ft.
2.0 M	6.6 ft.
1.5 M	4.9 ft.
1 M	3.3 ft.
.9 M	35.4 in.
.6M	23.6 in.
.5 M	19.7 in.
.3M	11.8 in.
.2M	7.9 in.

Index

Numbers in **bold** refer to pages with illustrations

A

accidents
    assistance at sea, 139
    causes of, 9, 49
    missing vessels, 140
    right-of-way concept, 11
action to avoid collisions,
        18–**19**, 55–57
aground vessels
    lights and shapes, **40**, 89–90
    sound signals, 32, 95, 96
air-cushion vessels, **34**, 82
Alaska demarcation line, 119,
        136
all-around lights
    colors and visibility, **33**,
        80–81
    defined, 32, 79
    exemptions, 98
    positioning and spacing, 101
    screens for, 103
alternative compliance proce-
        dures, 141–43
anchored vessels
    lights and shapes, **38, 40**, 70,
        89–90, 102
    sound signals, **32**, 95, **96**
Andrea Doria, 17–18, 55
applicability of Rules, 9, 13,
        43–45
    Inland Rules, 113, 143–44
    lights and shapes, 44, 45, 78
    multiple vessels, 11, 25
    oar-driven vessels, 22
    racing rules versus, 14
assistance at sea, 139
assistance to marine casualties,
        139
Atlantic Coast demarcation line
    Fifth District, 117, 122–23
    First District, 117, 119–21
    Seventh District, 117, 123–27
avoiding collisions, 18–**19**,
        55–**57**

B

barges, 96, 113–15, 116
bays, 13
bearings
    compass, 17, 53, 54
    radar, 76
    relative, 16–**17, 54**–55
bells, 91, 111
bends and blind areas, 20, 31,
        58, 60, 92–93
blasts, short and prolonged,
        90–91
bow wave surfing, 23
breadth, 47, 48
broken down vessels. *See* com-
        mand, vessels not under

C

Calamai, Captain, 17–18
canoes, 22, 85. *See also* human-
        powered vessels
cell phones, 31
Certificate of Alternative
        Compliance, 141–43
channels, narrow, 20, 30, 57–60, **59**
    human-powered vessels, 22
    Mr. Fission collision, 24
Charles Jourdan, 14
collisions
    sailboats while racing, 14
    taking head-on, 76
COLREGS. *See* international
        and inland rules
command, vessels not under
    defined, 12, 46, 48
    lights and shapes, **38**, 70,
        87–88
    responsibilities, 73–74
    sound signals, 95, **96**
communications. *See also* sig-
        nals, sounds and lights;
        VHF radios
    between boats, 42, 50, 72
    English requirement, 148
    head-on situations, 67–**68**
    helm to lookout, 50
    overtaking, 60
compass bearings, 17, 53, 54
composite units, 116
conversion table, 153

**Cooperative Vessel Traffic
        Service, 151**
course changes, 18–**19**, 56–**57**
crab boats, 13, 48
crossing situations, 69–**70**
    narrow channels, 59
    overtaking versus, 25, 65
    power-driven vessels, 27
    sound signals, **31, 94**

D

danger signal, 72
day shapes. *See* lights and shapes
decision tree, 19, inside front
        cover
definitions, 12–13, 46–48, 90–91
demarcation lines
    Alaska, 119, 136
    Atlantic Coast, Fifth District,
        117, 122–123
    Atlantic Coast, First District,
        117, 119–21
    Atlantic Coast, Seventh
        District, 117, 123–27
    Gulf Coast, Eighth District,
        118, 129–32
    Gulf Coast, Seventh District,
        117, 127–29
    Pacific Coast, Eleventh
        District, 118, 133
    Pacific Coast, Thirteenth
        District, 118, 134–35
    Pacific Coast, Twelfth
        District, 118, 134
    Pacific Islands, 118, 136
    Puerto Rico and Virgin
        Islands, 117, 127
    purpose of, 13, 44, 119
distress signals, **41**, 97, 112
diving operations, **38**, 87–88
draft constraints
    crossing situations, 70
    defined, 12, 47, 48
    lights and shapes, **39**, 70, 88
    responsibilities between ves-
        sels, 73–74
    sound signals, 95, **96**
dredging operations, **38**, 87,
        102, 115
dual watch VHF-FM radios, 147

E

Endeavor, 14

F

fairways, 20, 57–60
fishing gear, 13
fishing vessels
    crossing situations, 70
    defined, 12, 46, 48
    lights and shapes, 37, 86,
        102–3, 107
    narrow channels, 57, 58–59
    as power boats, 13
    responsibilities, 73–74
    sound signals, 95, **96**
    traffic separation schemes,
        61–62
flashing lights, 32, **33**, **41**, 79–81,
    80, 112
fog
    lookouts, 49–50
    precautions for, 17–18
    safe speed and, 52, 76
    visibility restrictions, 29

G

give-way vessels
    collision avoidance, 18–**19**,
        56–**57**
    crossing situations, 27, 69, 70
    defined, 12
    obligations of, 11, 71, **72**
    overtaking, 65
gongs, 91, 111
Granholm, 15, 49
Great Lakes
    applicability of Rules, 13
    crossing situations, 27
    defined, 47
    head-on situations, 26
    Vessel Bridge-to-Bridge
        Radiotelephone Act
        exemptions, 149
Gribbin, Captain William,
    30–31
Gulf Coast demarcation line
    Eighth District, 118, 129–32
    Seventh District, 117, 127–29

H

head-on situations, 26–27,
    67–**68**, 76
high-speed craft, 106
hovercraft, **34**, 82
human-powered vessels
    applicability of Rules, 13, 22
    lights, **36**, 85
    maneuverability restrictions,
        22–23
    narrow channels, 22
    negligent operation, 23
    traffic separation schemes, 22

I

injuctions, 139–40
injuries, 139
Inland Rules. *See* international
    and inland rules
inshore traffic zones, **21**
international and inland rules.
    See also applicability of
    rules
    alternative compliance proce-
        dures, 141–43
    familiarity with, 9
    learning, 10
    purpose of, 11, 22
    requirements to carry copy
        of, 9, 113
International Code of Signals,
    112
International Maritime
    Organization, 9, 61
International Regulations for
    the Prevention of Collision
    at Sea. See international
    and inland rules
International Yacht Racing
    Rules (IYRR), 14

K

kayaks
    applicability of Rules, 13, 22
    lights, **36**, 85
    maneuverability restrictions,
        22–23
    narrow channels, 22
    negligent operation, 23
    traffic separation schemes, 22

L

law enforcement vessels, **34**, 113
legal citations, 152
length, 47, 48, 145
lights and shapes
    alternative compliance proce-
        dures, 14–43
    applicability of Rules, 44, 45, 78
    colors and visibility of lights,
        32–**33**, **80**–81, 103–5
    course changes and naviga-
        tion lights, 56, 57
    definitions, 32, **33**, 79–**80**
    exemptions, 98–99, 113
    installation, 106
    intensity of lights, 104
    pecking order of vessels,
        28–**29**, 74
    positioning and spacing,
        100–106
    shapes requirements, 103
lights and shapes by vessel type
    aground, **40**, 89–90
    anchored, **38**, **40**, 70, 89–90,
        102
    barges, 113–15, 116
    diving operations, **38**, 87–88
    draft restrictions, **39**, 70, 88
    dredging operations, **38**, 87,
        102, 115
    fishing, 37, 86, 102–3, 107
    law enforcement, 34
    maneuverability restrictions,
        38, 87–88
    not-under-command, **38**, 70,
        87–88
    oar-driven vessels, **36**, 85
    pilot, **39**, 89
    power-driven, **34**, 80, 82,
        100–106
    sailing, **36**, **80**, 85
    towing and pushing, **35**,
        83–84, 87
lights for signalling. *See* signals,
    sounds and lights
lobster boats, 13, 48
lookouts, 49–50
    radar versus, 50
    sailing vessels, 15, 50
lost vessels, 140

M

maneuverability restrictions
defined, 12, 46–47, 48
kayaks, 22–23
lights and shapes, **38**, 87–88
responsibilities between vessels, 73–74
sound signals, 95, **96**
maneuvering and warning signals, **31**, 59–60, 72, 92–94
maneuvering lights, 106
marine casualties, 139
masthead lights
colors and visibility, **33**, 80–81
defined, 32, 79
exemptions, 98, 99
high speed craft, 106
positioning and spacing, 100–101
screens for, 103
meeting situations
sailing vessels, **28**, 63–**64**
sound signals, **31**, 94
Merchant Ship Search and Rescue Manual, 112
mine-clearing operations, 38, 87, 88
missing vessels, 140
motorsailing versus sailing, 13, 74
Mr. Fission, 24, 49

N

Navigation Rules, International-Inland, 9
negligent operations, 23, 138–40
non-electric lights, 105
not-under-command vessels.
See command, vessels not under

O

oar-driven vessels
applicability of Rules, 13, 22
lights, **36**, 85
maneuverability restrictions, 22–23
narrow channels, 22

negligent operation, 23
traffic separation schemes, 22
ocean-liners, 13
oceans, 13
overtaking, 24–**25**, 65–**66**
crossing versus, 25, 65
Granholm v. TFL Express, 15
sailing vessels, 14, 63
sound signals, **31**, 59–60, 94

P

Pacific Coast demarcation line
Eleventh District, 118, 133
Thirteenth District, 118, 134–35
Twelfth District, 118, 134
Pacific Islands demarcation line, 118, 136
pecking order of vessels, 28–**29**, 74
penalties
negligent operations, 138–40
violation of Rules, 137–38
pilot vessels
lights and shapes, **39**, 89
sound signals, **96**
power-driven vessels
crossing situations, 69–**70**
defined, 12, 46, 48, 145–46
fishing boats as, 13
head-on situations, 67–**68**
kayaks versus, 23
lights and shapes, **34**, 80, 82, 100–106
responsibilities, 73–74
sailboats as, 13
sound signals, 95, **96**
prolonged blast, 90–91
public safety activities, 113
Puerto Rico and Virgin Islands demarcation line, 117, 127
purse seine vessels, 45, 107
pushing vessels. *See* towing and pushing vessels

R

racing sailboats, 14
radar, 30, 50, 51–53
radar bearings, 76

radar reflectors, 30
radios. *See* VHF radios
radiotelephones. *See* VHF radios
reciprocal course, 67, 68
reciprocal heading, 68
relative bearings, 16–**17**, **54**–55
responsibilities between vessels, 28–**29**, 73–74
responsibility to avoid collisions, 14, 45–46
right-of-way
concept of, 11
International Yacht Racing Rules, 14
risk of collisions, 16, 53–55, **54**
Andrea Doria sinking, 17–18, 55
relative bearings, 16–**17**
rowboats. *See* oar-driven vessels
Rules of the Road. *See* international and inland rules

S

sailing vessels
collision while racing, 14
defined, 12, 13, 28, 46, 48, 63
lights and shapes, **36**, 80, 85
lookouts, 15, 50
meeting situations, **28**, 63–**64**
motorsailing versus sailing, 13, 74
narrow channels, 57, 58
overtaking, 14, 63
responsibilities, 73–74
sound signals, 95, **96**
tacks, **28**, 63, **64**
Sealnes, 24, 49
seaplanes, **40**, 46, 73, 90
Security Broadcast Systems, 42
Sersou, 26–27
short blast, 90–91
sidelights, **80**
colors and visibility, 33, 80–81
defined, 32, 79
exemptions, 98
positioning and spacing, 101, 102
screens for, 103

signals, sounds and lights
  alternative compliance proce-
    dures, 141–43
  to attract attention, 97
  definitions, 90–91
  distress signals, **41**, 97, 112
  equipment requirements, 91,
    98, 99, 108–11
  law enforcement vessels, 113
  maneuvering and warning
    signals, **31**, **59**–60, 72,
    92–94
  narrow channels, 20
  public safety activities, 113
  VHF radios versus, 42
  visibility restrictions, **32**,
    95–**96**
Silver Isle, 26–27
single-handed sailors, 15, 50
Smith, Captain E. J., 16
speed
  collision avoidance, 18, 56
  safe speed, 15–16, 51–53
  Titanic, 16
  visibility restrictions and, 51,
    52, 76
stand-on vessels
  collision avoidance, 18–**19**,
    56–**57**
  crossing situations, 27, 69, 70
  defined, 12
  obligations of, 11, 71–**72**
steaming lights. *See* masthead
  lights
sternlights, 32, **33**, 79–81, **80**
Stockholm, 17–18
strobe lights, 97
submarines, **34**, 44, 45

T
TFL Express, 15, 49
Titanic, 16, 52
towing and pushing vessels
  as composite units, 116
  defined, 146
  lights and shapes, **35**, 83–84,
    87
  maneuverability restrictions,
    47, 48, 87

sound signals, 32, 95, **96**
  visibility restrictions, 95, **96**
  whistles, 111
traffic separation schemes
  (TSS), **21**, 60–**62**
  crossing, **20**, 21, 60
  establishment of, 44, 45
  fishing boats in, 61–62
  human-powered vessels, 22
  rowboats, 23
trawling vessels, 13, 107
trolling, 13

U
underway, 12, 47, 48
United States Inland Rules. *See*
  international and inland
  rules
U.S. Coast Guard
  Security Broadcast Systems,
    42
  Web site for navigation rules, 9

V
Vessel Bridge-to-Bridge
  Radiotelephone Act, 31, 42,
  145–49. *See also* VHF
  radios
  applicability of, 145
  definitions, 145–46
  exemptions, 148–49
  legal citations, 152
  purpose of, 145
vessel constrained by her draft.
  See draft constraints
vessel engaged in fishing. *See*
  fishing vessels
vessel not under command. *See*
  command, vessels not
  under
vessel reporting requirements,
  140
vessel restricted by her ability to
  maneuver. *See* maneuverability restrictions
vessels
  defined, 12, 46
  more than two, 11, 25
  pecking order of vessels,
    28–29, 74

vessels in sight of one another,
  62–74
vessel traffic services (VTS), 21,
  24, 146, 150–51
VHF radios. *See also* Vessel
  Bridge-to-Bridge
  Radiotelephone Act
  contacting unknown vessels,
    42, 55
  designated frequencies, 42,
    147
  dual watch capabilities, 147
  English requirement, 148
  failure of, 148
  frequency requirement,
    146–47
  maintenance of, 148
  requirements for, 146–47
  signal coverage, 42
  use of, 31, 42, 50, 94, 148
violation of Rules, 137–38
visibility restrictions, 29–30,
  75–77
  defined, 12
  lookouts, 49–50
  safe speed and, 51, 52, 76
  sound signals, **32**, 95–**96**
visual contact between vessels,
  62–74

W
warning signals. *See* maneuvering and warning signals
waterways, 13
Web site for navigation rules, 9
Western Rivers
  applicability of Rules, 13
  crossing situations, 27
  defined, 47
  head-on situations, 26
  whistles, 90–91, 108–11
Wing-in-Ground (WIG) craft,
  12, 73, 82, 90